Understanding Christina I
for A Level OCR Poetry

Another Gavin's Guide for A Level students and their teachers

By Gavin Smithers

Another of **Gavin's Guides**- study books packed with insight. They aim to help you raise your grade!

Understanding Christina Rossetti's Poems for A Level OCR Poetry is a complete study guide, written for students and teachers preparing for A level exams in 2019 and subsequent years.

Series editor: Gill Chilton

You will need a copy of the poems:

Selected Poems of Christina Rossetti (Wordsworth Editions) Available on Amazon.

CONTENTS

Introduction

Christina Rossetti's poems- or rather, three very different and distinctive selections from them- feature in the specifications for English Literature A-Level of OCR, WJEC and Edexcel. Each exam board has, for their own reasons, made a different choice of poems. In this Gavin's Guide we are studying the 15 poems selected by OCR.

We can infer from this that Rossetti was and is a significant poet, both in her own time and now- that some of the issues she raises still strike a chord with us a century and a quarter after her death. Because we live in a much **more secular society** than she did, those issues are- for today's reader- less to do with her religious instincts and more about **gender and equality** between men and women.

She was a prolific poet, and she used a wide range of forms, styles and voices, from very short lyrics to long narrative poems; sonnets and ballads feature prominently in her work.

Stylistically, she uses **rhyme, repetition and symbolism** to create a sense of the concrete; the poems seem solid, like Victorian masonry. But their apparent simplicity is a trap for the unwary. There is a fascinating degree of **ambiguity** in many of the poems, which seem to have **hidden meanings** for those readers who are alert enough to detect them.

Rossetti herself felt some conflict between the pressures of **conventional Victorian mores** and behaviour, with its **deprecation of women, its patriarchal values and its authoritarianism**, and what we recognise as a more **romantic and feminist** instinct.

All of these strands come together in "Goblin Market", where predatory male characters clash with brave and not-so-demure young heroines. The poem throws into its recipe female modesty and immodesty, an ethos of sin, punishment and death, the **exploitation of women** by men, and **the ability of women to retaliate**; it seems to advocate a more feminine culture, and it emphasises that mistakes should be forgiven, not punished- in particular when they arise from curiosity.

Her religious beliefs drive her personal values- God, and godliness, are never far away- and there is a **moral seriousness** about her which repeatedly eschews "vanity"; it ultimately finds true meaning more in her relationship with God than in her dealings with men or friends ("Twice" is the best example of this). This approach may be at least in part a way of dealing with **acute loneliness**; her illnesses in the later part of her life made her increasingly reclusive and sober-minded, so we would expect her later poems to meditate extensively on **human isolation and spirituality**.

This fundamental seriousness of purpose, though, does not exclude a certain **playfulness**; in some of the poems there is a childlike simplicity and **sense of fun**, very different from the brooding, heavy intensity of her late religious poems.

You might think that we are dealing with a poet very much rooted in the Victorian age; but there is something in these poems which makes them relevant and able to speak to us in our **post-feminist** world too. The earlier critical reception they received reflected a tendency at that time to judge the poems less on their own merit and more **as poems written by a woman**; it also found them less ambiguous and much less **subversive** than we do today.

It is interesting, however, that there is still plenty of analysis being published which misses the darker ambivalences and ambiguities in many of the poems.

A lingering, sentimental view of Rossetti as a lyrical romantic somehow encourages a **superficial** reading of the poems, and misses the sharpness of her intellect and her **(often passionate) arguments in favour of social and educational reform** which would benefit women in particular.

The challenge we face is to arrive at **a balanced, broadly-based and accurate understanding** and judgment of what Christina Rossetti was aiming to say in her poetry, and- and this is a different critical point entirely- to determine how the poems speak to us today. Just as the responses of her first readers and critics were shaped by the traditions and cultures they knew, contemporary responses to these poems- both now and in future generations- will continue to change, and be motivated in (and limited by) the **cultural climate** which influences how we read them.

The danger for today's reader is that, because we live in a secular and, to some extent at least, equality- based culture, we may find the religiosity and piety of some of the poems unpalatable; it seems naive. This is why only two of the fifteen poems for OCR are overtly religious or devotional ("Good Friday", "Soeur Louise de la Misericorde").

The selection of poems you are given is chosen well, to invite you to find relevant themes for today. We learn a great deal, in reading them, about Victorian attitudes, but **the moral and practical issues about how men and women should behave towards each other** never cease to be topical.

Perhaps the most intriguing interpretative issue concerns the poems' critique of what it is to be a woman (in a man's world); **do the poems accept, rebel against, or undermine the status quo?**

How should you approach your study?

The assessment objectives are the key. Your Rossetti study will contribute 20% of your overall A-level mark.

The weightings are 10% each for AO1 and AO3, meaning that you are expected to **have something sensible, and thoughtful**, and of your own, **to say, that you say it effectively**, and that you show that you understand how **the culture and era Rossetti wrote in, and the culture and era you are studying the poems in, affect our interpretations of the poems.**

AO2 gets 7.5% of the marks here- you must show how Rossetti creates meaning; this will come from your close reading of the poems and your analysis of her methods.

AO4 contributes 5%- this is to do with identifying and commenting on connections across literary texts, which will include making comparisons of themes or characterisation in Rossetti and in your drama text.

The drama and poetry pre-1900 paper therefore adds up to 40% of the A-level, once you allow for the Shakespeare play too.

In this guide, I address the AOs, so that I hope that, in reading it, you will be stimulated to formulate more ideas of your own, and that you will be confident in your own analysis of the poems.

Your exam essay will require you to write about the treatment of **a theme** in your poetry and drama texts. The question will be **broadly based**, so that your ability to evaluate writers' treatment of a topic can be judged. Specimen topics are **the presentation of love; the morality of sex; power and gender; prohibition; misunderstanding; social status.**

To take just one example- Rossetti explores what is forbidden in "Goblin Market", "Shut Out", "Maud Clare" and "From the Antique".

You should be able to take any of these topics- and make a list of your own, of other topics you detect in the poems- and then write practice essays, once you really know the poems. At the end of this study guide, I give you an example in Appendix 4, but I restrict the analysis to Rossetti because I can't tell which of the drama texts you will have studied. It could be one of a good number. The OCR website has extensive sample essays you can study for content and marking; please make sure you use this valuable resource.

Working through this Gavin's Guide

Christina Rossetti (1830-1904) lived a secluded life- partly due to ill-health, from 1872 onwards.

Her outlook was deeply influenced by her **lifelong attachment to the Anglican Church**, with its patriarchal attitude and its **implicit view that women are inferior to men** in many ways. Her poems embody or represent these conventional attitudes but at the same time they **criticise cultural and gender assumptions. They assert the right of Victorian women to a voice of their own, when they are otherwise repressed and patronised.**

In Appendix 1, I summarise the evolution of critical judgments of Rossetti and her poems, from the 19th century onwards. My personal view is that much of this evaluation has tended to underestimate her rebelliousness, her reluctance to conform; even though her religious beliefs militated against being too revolutionary, she is **consistent in her protests against how a male-led society disregards and disadvantages women.** You may find it useful to measure your own response to the poems against mine, and see where you think the evidence of the texts of the poems leads you.

A superficial, uncritical reading- in my view- will reveal only the conventional aspects of the thought which motivates the poems, and which they contain; **women being passive, and dominated by men, and living ultimately unfulfilled lives.** Such women, in these poems, are unhappy.

But an alternative view is persuasive- **Rossetti's women** are- as she herself is- driven to a self-sufficiency which makes them **reject inadequate, faithless or dominating men.** Her **narrators are often dead women, or women who have chosen to be alone** rather than social creatures, because of their experience of failed romantic hopes, male disregard, neglect or abandonment. They have suffered varying degrees of emotional betrayal, control and cruelty.

On this reading, **many of the poems are grounded in bitterness, and they seek to subvert the calm and complacent surface of a society which chooses to deny women the ambitions, desires and potential they have, purely on the grounds of their gender.** Some of Rossetti's poems have ghosts as narrators; the threat of haunting the living often weakens into a generous decision not to haunt, but it is significant that **settling scores or taking revenge is only possible once you are dead**.

It is legitimate to refer to elements of Rossetti's own life, where this helps us to understand her point of view. As with all writers, we need to **avoid the trap of the autobiographical fallacy; she is**

not writing in her own persona (although it has to be said that she does not always distance herself from the voice of her narrators to the extent Robert Browning or Tennyson do). What we know of Christina Rossetti's life is, however, relevant to her writing, and I summarise the basic information you need, in Appendix 2.

In Appendix 3, I list some of the key concepts which are important in the writing of the poems and the thinking behind them; some of the history of ideas here is highly relevant to understanding meaning in the poems.

The fifteen poems

Song: When I am dead, my dearest

This poem dates from 1848, and it was published in 1862. Rossetti therefore was **not writing it from the first-hand experience of being an embittered wife**, although this was the time of her unhappy engagement to James Collinson. In fact, the two characters in the poem- the narrator and the addressee- are not particularised at all. We know nothing about their ages or backgrounds, because the purpose here is not to tell a personal narrative but to use **archetypes** to broaden the poem, so that it can address the disparity between the romanticised, lazy acceptance of the conventions of marriage, and the empty gestures which go with it. They result in ongoing distress- for the female participant.

This strategy of archetyping is very characteristic of Rossetti. It universalises the issue of interpersonal relationships, and **the need (especially for a woman) to be able to speak**, evaluate and determine for yourself what a particular type of relationship means to you, especially when marriage is regarded as irrevocable and inescapable- "till death us do part".

The poem is therefore a contemplation and a warning of the potential **suffering an unsuitable marriage may commit women to**. The theme of **women who are denied or unable to achieve fulfilment**, and so excluded from realising their dreams, or even basic interpersonal happiness, recurs in several of the poems you study- for example, in "Shut Out" and "Twice".

In this case- as in **"Remember"**- **death is the means of escape from marital misery**, so the narrator looks forward to it. A grotesque reversal of the proper balance between life and death (life is to be enjoyed and death is unwelcome and to be feared) reflects the improper and **unanticipated misery the poem charts, of moving from being single to being well and truly married**. It is only at the very end of the poem that the female victim is able to assert herself, with a sharp and vicious twist of the knife; even when deprived of sight, hearing and touch, she will still be able to assert her right to forget her husband, and thus **destroy the possessive control** of the architect of her married misery.

At first sight, the form of the poem looks innocuous enough; it is a poem in two balanced octaves, each of which rhymes ABCBBDED, with a balanced repetition of "remember..... forget"; and with a polite, reserved tone and simple, calm diction.

The first stanza appears to exhort the survivor (the addressee) not to memorialise the narrator once she is dead- she does not want elaborate gestures of mourning (planting roses, as a **symbol of romantic love**, or a cypress tree, to create shade and peace). The narrator gives the addressee the freedom of choice, to remember or to forget her, as he pleases ("and if thou wilt"); he has freedom of will and choice, in this as in everything else. There is no injunction to mourn. The natural colour and dampness (grass, dewdrops and showers) is an adequate marker, and perhaps a more honest one, of a relationship in which real love was absent. Why should we make a fuss about commemorating something which does not deserve to be remembered?

A closer look at the language helps us to detect the tone and meaning. The alliteration of **dead/dearest, sing/sad songs,** and **green grass,** and the **repetition** of the permissive **"if thou wilt"** creates a note of **bitterness and sarcasm.** The surface impression is that this is a conventional poem setting the survivor free emotionally, but the underlying tone is resentful, and it says "I couldn't care less what you feel or don't feel, and I don't want any false and falsifying memorials".

The second stanza **shifts the focus** dramatically from the addressee (thou) to the speaker (I). The freedom and conditionality of the addressee's weak and uncommitted position contrasts with the narrator's clarity about her own perspective. Her sensory deprivation, by virtue of being dead (I shall not see/ feel/ hear) leaves her still in control of her will, and she will make her own decision about remembering and forgetting the addressee. Because the final word of the poem is **"forget"**, it is clear that **the narrator herself will not mourn the end of the relationship**.

Her perceptions are independent and subjective, and utterly unromantic- shadows instead of shady, rain instead of showers and dewdrops; **shadows and rain are hard and lacking in comfort** or emotional connotation. Her position is that, **though** dead, she will continue in a state between living and oblivion, "dreaming through the twilight".

The description of this twilight, and the introduction and presentation of the nightingale, reveal more about the tone and meaning of the poem. **The twilight** does not change- it does not "rise nor set"- it is a state of **permanent gloom or limbo**. **The nightingale sings "as if in pain"**- this is really **referred pain, the pain the narrator has felt** in her own relationship. The nightingale has a long symbolic value in literature, as the voice of beauty, joy and mourning; this narrator perceives the nightingale's song- which she hears habitually while she is alive, but will not hear once she is dead- as **the voice of her own unrelenting distress**.

The clinching and closing argument in the second stanza is this; the narrator's living experience will crystallise into a decision to forget the failed relationship with the man who was supposed to be- and still thinks he is- "my dearest", because **being dead gives her the freedom to choose** how to judge that relationship once it has ended (in just the same way the survivor can). The inference is that the writing of the poem is **a rebalancing of power**- it corrects the imbalance in which the reality of **the pain of the narrator is hidden beneath the apparently smooth, calm and conventional appearance of her marriage.**

Just as **the superficially submissive, restrained and polite narrative tone is a veil**, behind which there is something acidic, subversive and sarcastic, the poem itself becomes an artifice, a monument to a relationship which appears to be conventionally satisfactory, but is really a vehicle for so much pain that death is a welcome escape, and the only way to stop the passive suffering. **The relationship between the narrator and the addressee is framed in negative terms** (no...no....nor in stanza 1, not...not...not...not....nor in stanza 2); life above ground is less attractive and peaceful than death and being below ground, and the misery of continual exposure to shadows and rain is preferable to the continuing pain the nightingale articulates by night and day (it is thought to be a bird which never sleeps).

The **alliteration and repetition** in this poem is **superficially consoling and affectionate, but in fact it is bitter and menacing. The concept of pain is central to finding the meaning of the poem.**

The same approach drives the sonnet "Remember", which is not a conventional sonnet in its meaning; it expresses not love and gratitude but a hatred of male control and female subjugation.

Remember

This poem was written about a year after the one just referred to.

Using **the sonnet form as a protest against a loveless, oppressive marriage** takes the theme of female disempowerment further; it depicts the apparently respectable Victorian marriage as a travesty.

The rhyme scheme- ABBAABBA CDDECE- holds no surprises, although we should note the absence of a final, resolving rhyming couplet; and we can see the significance of **the ending, an injunction to "be sad".**

The poem appears to be bound together by five repetitions of "remember", the first three of them followed by the specific "me", the last two looser. **The poem is littered with pronouns-** me/I/you/me/I/me/you/me/you/me/you/you/me/I/ you/you. They are **arranged in an alternating or oppositional pattern, which hints at the conflict the sonnet alludes to.**

Again, there is no specific identifying of the speaker or the addressee, in terms of their age, gender or marital status. The use of **euphemism** abounds, partly in the **lexis of death and burial** (gone away/ far away/ silent land/ pray/ go/ darkness/

corruption/ sad), and partly in **the symbolic use of a journey to represent death** (the same applies in "Uphill", and in Hamlet's "To be or not to be" soliloquy).

Once again, the narrator anticipates **her own death**, and we cannot anticipate when it will come; she presents it **as an escape**, and the means of asserting her power, finally, in a relationship in which she has been oppressed.

The simple imagery in the octave defines that this is a relationship in which **the addressee has controlled the narrator; "you" planned "our future", which "you" tell me about, and "you" "hold me by the hand" repeatedly- a gesture of possession which has stopped "me" from leaving**, and has left death as the only means of escape.

The sestet asserts the narrator's unobtrusive power, and it twists the emotional knife in an unexpected (and satisfying) way. The trio of "remember me"s has seemed to be conciliatory and submissive, but **in the sestet the narrator introduces the concept of haunting her widower, whom she will force to "remember and be sad"**, provided that death leaves behind it any small capacity for her thoughts (of revenge) to have any effect on him. If he remembers her, he will have to accept the blame for what he has done (does this extend to motivating her to suicide?), and, while his remembering will not be accompanied by grief, it will be tinged with regret or sadness- so that, if he only remembers her for some of the time, he will experience some relief (forget and smile).

Her **repeated imperative "remember me……remember and be sad" is faintly menacing; it is almost a curse.**

The sonnet cleverly knits together the couple's past and the survivor's future. The nature of life after death (and any Christian version of it) is ignored, because it might lead to an incongruously cheerful tone. Instead, the architecture of this poem and of "When I am dead" is sketched, gloomily, from the accumulating of dark details- prayer, grief, darkness and sadness, and sad songs, cypress trees, showers, rain, dewdrops and twilight.

"Remember" is the more sophisticated poem because of the dimension that **the dead can haunt the living**. Whereas in "When I am dead", I can choose whether to remember or forget, when "I am gone away", I am **not so dead**, and I can perhaps direct back to the offender "a vestige of the thoughts that once I had".

The limited characterisation of the male character in "Remember" establishes him as a man who has put his wife through sessions of counselling and prayer, and has physically restrained her from leaving. He has made plans for her within the marriage, without any consideration of her. He has trapped her in a controlling and emotionally (if not physically) abusive relationship, and made it impossible for her to leave unless she dies. Victorian marriage law made it very difficult for women to escape abusive marriages.

When we read the sonnet from the point of view of a wronged and browbeaten wife, it is spoken trough gritted teeth, with menace and feeling. If, however, we read it from the point of view of the widower, we can make a case (even if it is a flimsy one, a pretence) that, as a sonnet, it is a love poem, a consolation, and a letting go. In other words, if we are culturally disposed to see the women we marry as obedient, dependent, and uncomplaining, we may expect them to let us go emotionally after they have died. On this reading, both poems place no obligation of remembrance or loyalty on the man, of the type a widow (for example, in a Jane Austen novel) might be expected to demonstrate.

Read together, the poems, as a pair, offer a coherent philosophy, in which they support and reinforce each other. **Marriage is convenient for men; they can be dominant in it, and can ignore their wives' pain and their needs for some identity of their own.** In the end, however, these women retain (even if only in dying, and thus making themselves unavailable) some resilience and autonomy, so that they can finally wriggle out from under male control. **Freedom from men enables**

women to breathe and to have their own identity. The marriages of Laura and Lizzie in "Goblin Market" are fantastically free from men, and are the better for it, although they are surreal.

These two poems, the first in the list you study, establish Rossetti's credentials as a feminist poet, alert to the restrictions and limitations gender roles have the potential to impose on women, especially within the Victorian concept of marriage.

In the poem An "Immurata" Sister, Rossetti observes that "**Men work and think, but women feel**", and this capacity for feeling often makes her female narrators exhausted or frustrated; to be a man would be simpler and so much easier!

On page 100 of Jan Marsh's "Christina Rossetti- a literary biography" (Jonathan Cape, 1994) the poem is printed with the variant in line 6 "our future that *we* planned" (my italics). This neutralises the poem completely, of course, but I have not seen it reproduced anywhere else.

From the Antique ("It's a weary life, it is, she said")

The third poem in your selection offers a female point of view, this time not on a personal relationship but on **women's wider**

experience of life. As in "When I am dead, my dearest", the words **not, none** and **nothing** populate the poem, to show what is wrong or missing or dysfunctional.

Again, the speaker is an **archetype- female**, we know, **and frustrated**, we know. She says that it would be better to be a man; and that it would be better to be "nothing at all", to be less than human, to be less noticeable than a drop of water or a grain of dust.

The form of the poem is like a hymn or a ballad. Stanza 1 has a rhyme scheme ABCB, and different numbers of syllables from line to line (9/9/9/10). The same applies in stanza 2, except that lines 6 to 8 each have one syllable fewer than the corresponding lines in stanza 1 (8/8/9). In stanza 3, the rhyme is still ABCB, and the syllable count is 8/7/8/8. In stanza 4, the rhyme scheme still applies and the syllables are 8/7/9/9. We can take **the consistency of the rhyme scheme as a representation of the world continuing in its undisturbed, impassive pattern**, and the varying line lengths and stresses within them as a reflection of the narrator's distress.

She **seeks invisibility because she feels utterly insignificant**. "A woman's lot" is to have a body and a soul, but to have no meaningful place in the natural order, since, without her, "the world" would carry on regardless, with its seasons and the activity of nature, and no one would mourn her disappearance.

The poem **ignores the role of women as mothers**, and we may feel that this weakens the argument that women are in the margins of nature. The comparison the poem seeks to make is between the role or profile of men and women; being a man is less wearying because men have profile and impact.

"The world" in general is complacent about this redundancy of women (line 16) and the issue is an "ancient" one; it has always been thus. The poem is thus **a challenge to Victorian society to re-examine the underused, undereducated resource- the female half of the population.**

The poem was written in 1854 but it was **not published in Rossetti's lifetime**. This points to a degree of weakness in it. Certainly, reading the poem leaves us feeling that it goes nowhere and resolves nothing. In one sense this is justified, as it highlights the stasis of women in society, but it is unsatisfactory as a poem because it offers no possible resolution. If your life as a woman is so tedious as to be unbearable, you will surely have something to say about how to change the imbalance of power and opportunity between men and women. And taking the role of motherhood out of the poem ignores a source of purpose which of course is not available to men.

There are aspects of the style of the poem which are also less than wholly successful. The slightly plaintive tone, the extensive, but not very focused, alliteration, and the clunky repetition (all in all/ in all the world/ I wish and I wish) are features of Rossetti's narrative and more playful poems; they undermine the attempt to achieve a serious point of view here, so that the poem risks being petulant rather than thought-provoking.

The experiment of using the poem to report what someone else thinks or says (line 1) is another qualified success at best. **Where Rossetti uses a first person narrator, she usually manages to create a distinctive voice.** Here, by attributing the feelings of inadequacy, frustrated effort and perhaps depression to a third person, the poem does not really commit itself to endorsing those feelings, and if the reader does not identify with the point of view then the poem will be unconvincing.

Echo

In Greek mythology Echo was a nymph who helped Zeus to conceal his infidelities by delaying his wife in conversation. Echo was punished, by being able not to initiate dialogue, but only to repeat the end of what was said to her. This led to her humiliation by the self-obsessed Narcissus, and she pined away until all that was left of her was her voice.

How far Rossetti engages with the myth is debatable, because, whereas Echo's love for Narcissus was unrequited, the final line of this poem tells a different story. **The echo here is more the disembodied echo or ghost of a sexual affair which is long over, but lives on in the narrator's memory and dreams.** The narrator is dying (line 14), so time is short; she uses **the repeated imperative** "Come" five times (the same number of times the imperative "remember" appears in "Remember") **to create an emotional intensity** in the first two stanzas which is remarkable, not least because the rhetorical aspects of the diction cannot weaken it.

While the poem is littered with conventional low-level symbols of loss and distress (silence/night/dream/ eyes/ tears/ bitter/ sweet/ cold/ death/ low/ long ago) the striking central image is of the door of Paradise opening, to admit newcomers to its charmed circle. Normally, we would envisage ourselves being admitted to a room by **going into it from the outside** (as Rossetti presents entering the grave in "Uphill"); here, though, the dreamer's "thirsting longing eyes" see someone else **coming into Paradise**- the lover with the bright eyes- and the consolation is that once you are in paradise you can't leave. This is not claustrophobic, but the permanent fulfilment of a romantic fantasy. We will find the same kind of emotional intensity in "A Birthday".

"Echo" is in three stanzas of six lines with an ABABCC rhyme scheme. Each stanza consists of a single sentence. If we combine the fourth and fifth lines of each stanza, we have a poem in iambic pentameters, but the metre is much looser, more fluid and lyrical, in stanza 1, with its less concrete, more liquid, dream-like surrealism. The effect of breaking the fourth iambic pentameter in each stanza into two separate lines is to vary the pace; the fourth lines break up the streams of imperatives and achieve a slower lyricism, using variety in the process (simile, imagery, repetition).

Rossetti is successful in deploying transferred epithets- a door cannot be slow and eyes cannot be thirsty. The oxymoronic "speaking silence", and the substitution of "finished" for something that is unfinished, in the narrator's mind, adds originality to the first stanza.

Line 9, with its talk of souls, may be an allusion to John Donne's great romantic poem "The Extasie", and the pun on "long" and "longing" is Donnean. The **ethereal quality of a meeting in Paradise of souls** is offset by the concrete (and intensifying) repetition of "sweet"(how….too….bitter) and by the **solid image of the door, which has the same force here as the building of the wall in "Shut Out".**

The third stanza uses different techniques again, to convey **an intense desire for something unattainable.** In six lines, we have no fewer than seven repetitions (come/ to me in dreams/ that I may/ pulse/ breath/ low/ long ago) but the stanza does not feel repetitive, because the language is so simple and direct. These **repetitions, together with the lexical links** between stanzas 1 and 3, do **create an echoing effect**, though it has nothing to do with the Greek myth.

This poem is **another expression of feminine dissatisfaction**. Romantic satisfaction cannot be recaptured in a dream. The concept of a fulfilling sexual relationship cut off (by the premature and sudden death of the male partner?) recurs in "Sister Maude", but its strategic purpose there is very different.

"Echo" is a very sophisticated and accomplished poem, not just because the technical devices Rossetti uses are so unobtrusive, but because, in its structural use of the past and the present, and in its sense of the ebb and flow- of relationships, of emotional intensity, of time, of life and death- it manages to create a sense of continuity, and of context, in which a **thwarted love** (whether Echo's, or any female protagonist's) **defines the whole life experience of a woman- because "women feel".**

Shut Out

A good piece of research to shed light on this poem, and attune yourself to its use of symbolism, is for you to read two poems by William Blake-"London" and "The Garden of Love".

Blake's extraordinarily simple, hymn-like forms contain the most striking imagery and symbolism. Symbolic meanings- for example, what he intends by the marriage hearse- are not explained, but there is a sense that the helpless (infants, child chimney-sweeps, young prostitutes) and the exploited (soldiers) are victimised by the society and the Empire they happen to be born in.

The world Blake constructs in these two poems lacks both social and moral justice, and institutions like the Church and the monarchy are to blame. The lack of context or explanations makes Blake's symbols more even resonant and powerful. Rossetti does something similar here, with the disturbing building of the wall by the unresponsive, authoritarian "spirit".

Rossetti's poem is in seven stanzas of four lines with an ABBA rhyme scheme and eight syllables in every line- like a song, a hymn or a nursery rhyme. The regularity of this pattern implies that **what is in the poem is settled and non-negotiable; the narrator's protests are futile.**

The narrator is exiled from her garden. Although she hopes to regain access to it in the future (line 16), her request for a twig or some buds, to maintain her connection with it, is met with the further sanction of building a wall which removes any residual view of the lost world of "my delightful land".

Her ownership of the garden is important to her (my/mine/mine/my home/ my delightful land; lines 3,8,15, 24) because it turns the garden into something precious and more special than other gardens (lines 27-28). The final stanza shows us that the narrator has no capacity to enjoy nature except where she owns it. Do we judge this as a selfish, egomaniac and unworthy emotional reaction, and so label her outburst of frustration in stanza 6 a tantrum? No; we tend to sympathise, because the blank unresponsiveness and lack of empathy from the "shapeless spirit" seems harsh and cruel.

The spirit occupies the centre of the poem (stanzas 3-5) and will not be dislodged from his post. The inaction is masterful; he does not speak, but simply remains "blank and unchanging", and then builds the wall, thoroughly, remorselessly, dispassionately.

The closing two stanzas **switch from the past tense to the present. But the narrator's alienation, exclusion and distress continue unabated.** Here we have a dramatised version of the point made in "From the Antique"- men have authority, and, if you are a woman, men build walls that exclude you from your dreams, and **men treat you as a nonentity**.

Because we are familiar with the concept of the Garden of Eden, and Adam and Eve's exclusion from it as a consequence of their search for knowledge, it may be tempting to see the garden here as an allegory of that Garden. But there is no Adam here; Eve did not feel she owned the Garden of Eden; and there is no sense that the narrator has lost her garden as some kind of justified punishment. She can still observe birds and flowers in stanza 7, and she acknowledges that they have some appeal, but not the personal meaning and relevance of the garden she has lost.

Perhaps we should read Rossetti's poem in the light of Blake's treatment of the Garden of Love- a place which has lost its meaning for him, because it has been **built over by authoritarian concepts** (of sin and death). The Garden of Love used to be an innocent playground for him, but others (or experience) have turned it into something else.

If **the garden is a symbol of a poet's personal hopes and ambitions**, it may be that Rossetti is recording and processing her decision to withdraw from **the garden of earthly pleasures-** including the quest for personal romantic and sexual satisfaction. The poem was written in 1854, by which time the difficulty of reconciling her religious beliefs with proposals of marriage by Collinson had become apparent to her.

We can interpret the poem more broadly, however. What are women excluded from? They have no vote, no public profile, no career outside the home; this narrator feels "outcast" or excluded from what used to belong to her- her former home. Perhaps this poem, too, is **dramatizing the experience of marriage. The narrator might be Maude Clare, or Nell, or any woman disillusioned by unhappy marriage, or teetering on the brink of committing herself**, but inclined to avoid the irreversible leaving behind of the happy life she has enjoyed while she stayed in the garden.

On this reading, this poem is **another commentary on the institution of marriage, and how it deprives women of ownership of anything private or personal to them.**

In the Round Tower at Jhansi

According to the Illustrated London News in September 1857, a Captain Skene had shot his wife and then himself when surrounded by mutineers in the Indian Mutiny. In 1875, Rossetti added a note to the poem to the effect that the incident had been reported inaccurately; the Skenes had in fact been captured and murdered by the mutineers.

Rossetti tried unsuccessfully to enrol as a nurse for the Crimean War, so she was engaged in and sympathetic to the casualties of war generally.

The poem is in the form we are becoming familiar with- four-line stanzas rhyming ABAB. We may expect a poem about military conflict to involve men, and, perhaps, to be conventionally patriotic- although intelligent poets like Tennyson (in the celebrated "Charge of the Light Brigade") could celebrate heroism and condemn military incompetence at the same time.

Rossetti adopts a **highly dramatic approach to the narrative**, which is almost monosyllabic in its rush; there is no time to escape, but there is (just) time to face death with heroism and dignity. The fact that the reader has to attribute the dialogue to the respective characters, because it is not signposted for us, is a way of involving us more closely in the final two stanzas.

With the exception of the expository first stanza, the basic pattern is seven syllables in a line. **As time runs out, the lines become shorter.**

This opening stanza presents the mob in a way which slightly resembles the goblins in "Goblin Market"; they are numerous, noisy, animalistic, and getting closer. The fact that they are "below" implies that there is still a buffer of physical distance, but line 2 emphatically rules out any chance of escape. The multiplication in a fraction of a second, from a hundred to a thousand, and the repetition of "gained", are dramatic. Defining them as "wretches" makes it clear that our sympathies should not lie with these virtual animals.

The focus shifts, with line 5, to Skene and Mrs Skene, who is identified only as "his ....wife"; the description of her as young and pale is a brush stroke which creates **a sense of pathos**. We ask ourselves how a naïve and vulnerable young woman can have come to be exposed to this crisis. The answer is, presumably, that her devotion to him made her reckless of the danger in accompanying him on active service.

She speaks first, and he confirms her fear and her perception that they face imminent death. The emphasis on (their) youth is repeated, but now she is vibrant, not pale. The characters, like the reader, are lost for words as they take in their fate.

Just as we had a triad of "gained" in stanza one, we find "close" three times in stanza three. These repetitions create **a complex sense of protectiveness, intimacy and resoluteness**. The authorial intervention in line 12 does not make it clear who "them" is- the Skenes, who are about to kill themselves, or the mutineers, who motivate them to do so.

Stanza 4 opens with a second question from her to him (about the pain of being shot) and a mutual declaration of courage and self-sacrifice. The point is that **a defenceless young woman is as capable of the masculine virtues of extreme courage (in adversity) as any man.**

The final stanza starts with a moment of romantic intimacy which is poignant because it cannot last. The farewells in the closing line sustain the closeness and mutuality in their language which the couple have demonstrated in lines 6, 14 and 15.

The effect is that **we resist the subordinating of the "pale young wife" to the courage of a husband** of whom such behaviour is to be expected. There is no self-pity or recrimination from her, and in lines 15-16 she is as brave as him, despite her femininity.

Following the dismantling of the British Empire, we may now be accustomed to post-Colonial criticism, which explores and makes judgments about the values, assumptions, prejudices and abuses of power that go with the suppression of one culture by another.

Is there any of this instinct in Rossetti's poem? Presumably not, as this post-Colonial perspective would not have been a coherent approach or voice in her own time. I think she saw herself writing a poem based on what she believed was a factual news report; what she was interested in was **the potential for**

the pale young wife to behave as heroically as the army captain she had married.

Mrs Skene is a model of self-sacrifice; just as Lizzie sets out in "Goblin Market" to share the experience of decline and death which her sister appears to have brought upon herself.

A Birthday

The form and structure of this poem are similar to "Song- When I am dead, my dearest"- two balanced stanzas of eight lines, with a shift in the perspective or point of view in the second stanza. Just as, there, the final word of the earlier poem – "forget"- also occupies the same position at the end of the first stanza, there is a **structural repetition** here of "my love is come to me".

The regularity of the metre gives the poem a song-like quality (it is a type of hymn to God) and the confidence and certainty that the world of the saved soul is a reassuring one; the second stanza explores **the cultural and historical symbolism** of the Christian Church. The form and structure of the poem are themselves an expression of confidence that religious faith has substance, although it has no solid physical evidence other than some widely understood symbols appropriated by Christianity in its cultural history.

This is a straightforwardly lyrical poem which uses three **similes and then a series of images** about precious, delicate and rich objects to evoke romantic, or, more importantly, spiritual love in an optimistic, breathless way.

The similes in the first stanza are extended in an interesting way- the adjectives (singing/watered/thickset/halcyon) are deployed to create a sense of abundance, healthiness and a richness of joy. Birds, apple trees and seashells can be applied in similes to mean different things; in "An Apple Gathering" Rossetti uses a barren apple tree, whose fruit has been blighted or taken, as a symbol of loneliness and romantic isolation.

The word "halcyon" here means calm or tranquil; it is also a transferred epithet, in that the narrator's mood is idyllically happy.

After three subordinate clauses, each ending with a semi-colon, the stanza ends with **a comparative adjective (gladder) which intensifies or uplifts the three feel-good similes into a trinity of joyousness**. The source of joy is not the fact that is the narrator's birthday, but the fact that "my love is come to me", which represents some form of commitment or breakthrough, or, most likely, a personal epiphany or revelation.

The fact that the title of the poem is so **unspecific** points us towards a **metaphorical or non-literal** meaning.

The closing two lines of the first stanza also qualify **the narrator's joy,** in that they make it the product of, or **dependent upon, the action of another being** (my love). Attributing to the entity or being so far identified only as "my love" this power to generate joy in another person alerts us to the possibility that we are not reading about a human relationship here, but about a spiritual one.

There is still no birthday cake, card or present in the second stanza. Instead, the narrator moves on from the descriptive similes to issue a **sequence of imperatives** (Raise/ Hang/ Carve/ Work), all of which demand the producing of an elegant and extravagant wooden dais to commemorate the occasion. "Vair" is a medieval squirrel- fur used in heraldry; it takes its place in a procession of soft and exotic substances   (silk/ down/ vair/ doves) which turns into a list of precious and delicate items available only to royalty or the **very rich** (purple/pomegranates/ peacocks/ gold/ silver/ (gold)leaves/ silver fleurs-de-lys).

There is **an Old Testament feel** to much of this language. Pomegranates are associated with temples and high priests in the Old Testament and in medieval religious painting they are linked with Christ's suffering and resurrection. In **early Christian art**, the peacock, with its all-seeing eyes, symbolises the Church or God; more generally it has cultural connotations with immortality.

The fleur-de-lis is (like vair) a heraldic emblem. It is a representation of a lily and historically we associate it with the monarchy of and the nation of France. It has been adopted on coats of arms by towns all over the world. In **Christian religious art**, the fleur-de-lis is associated with purity and chastity, with Mary and with the Holy Trinity.

The second stanza commissions an elaborate artefact whose detail reflects the narrator's **sense of spiritual enrichment. The similes in the first stanza are from the secular or natural world, but the detail in the second stanza is more specifically a representation of spiritual belief.**

The penultimate line of the poem fits with this view; a birthday becomes "the birthday of my life", i.e the day on which I am born into (eternal) life- an event which happens on the day we are born, but not on any other birthday or anniversary. The second and third iteration of "is come", in line 16, and the conflation of my love….my life…my love, is another pointer to a religious, not a romantic, meaning for the poem.

The non-literal (metaphorical) style and the nature of the symbolism in stanza two are sufficiently unambiguous to permit us to conclude that this poem is prompted by the joy and security a Christian feels. While **religious faith is presented here as exotic and infinitely rich**, other later poems of Rossetti's understandably deal with other aspects of the Christian's view of the world- some of them are **less comfortable**. For now, though, this narrator feels that her conviction of security in the Church makes her immeasurably rich, in spiritual rather than literally material terms.

Maude Clare

This poem is **a ballad; traditionally a form in which a story is told and something tragic happens.** There are often gothic, as well as melodramatic, undertones.

Rossetti uses this style in some of her most famous poems- "Jessie Cameron", "Cousin Kate" and "Sister Maude". All of them depict **love gone bad**, and they explore **inconstancy, betrayal, sexual opportunism and the morality of sex.** This is the world of Thomas Hardy, who empathises with his poor, powerless victims, because they have so little economic or sexual power. Rossetti's ballads go further; they explore **female**

reactions to female jealousies and betrayals as well as those of men.

We know something about the history of this poem because it exists in manuscript in a form three and a half times as long. That poem is more in the manner of Keats' longer narrative poems, and it lacks the confidence we find, in the shorter version we study, that the reader can be trusted to work out where our sympathies should lie. In the longer, earlier version of the poem, Thomas marries for money and the rejection of Maude Clare is morally wrong; she is to be sympathised with, and she is almost idolised. The version we have is **more gritty, and more realistic**. The history of these two women's relationships with Thomas is not explored; the question is what should or can be done with **conventional views of marriage and the roles men and women are expected to adopt in it.** Thomas' long gaze at Maude Clare before he finally kisses Nell may be a gesture of defiance, of reluctant submission (to his mother's wishes), or a way of confirming to Maude Clare that his desire still lies with her. The poem as we have it argues both that **emotional dishonesty** is a flimsy basis for a marriage and that **the latitude and control given to men and husbands may be ineffectual, misguided, and in no-one's best interests.** The arguing and the lucidity comes, with linguistic precision, from the two women in this love triangle; the man is unable to express himself.

"Maude Clare" is in twelve stanzas of four lines, with an ABCB rhyme scheme. Rossetti uses varieties of this pattern in her other ballads too; it creates rhythmic and narrative dynamism. This is particularly interesting here, because so much of the poem is in the form of speech rather than action (37 of the 48 lines).

As in "Remember", there is **an embittered woman here; only this time it is not the narrator**, but a character in the poem. The poems share the theme of bitterness arising from romantic disappointment, and the powerlessness of many (most?) women to achieve satisfactory long-term relationships with men.

Maude Clare thought that the local squire, Thomas, would marry her- she was deceived and betrayed because he has just married Nell. In standing outside the church, to confront Thomas, his mother and his bride with his faithlessness, in an attempt to shame or humiliate him, **Maude Clare is quite modern, feisty and assertive!** We side with her, as the wronged party, but there is an **unexpected change of emphasis in the closing two stanzas where Nell expresses a (probably misplaced) confidence that she can make Thomas love her "best of all"** through perseverance and the passage of time (but

43

her new husband looks like a sexual opportunist and a serial philanderer).

Maude Clare has the same directness and lack of diplomacy as Jessie Cameron (a careless, fearless girl…..outspoken……somewhat heedless with her tongue/ And apt at causing pain), whose intransigence leads her to drown. But she stands for integrity, and against hypocrisy, as she sees it. **Having been rejected, she delivers her own rejection, in as provocative and shaming way as she can.** Nell's generosity, naïve as it may be, deprives her of the last word, which is what Maude Clare surely wanted most. The poem presents women with the dilemma that, because men may be programmed to be unfaithful (an accepted Victorian belief), **marriage always involves that unmanageable risk.**

All four characters- Thomas, his mother, Nell and Maude Clare- are **"pale"-** an adjective which recurs in five successive lines (11-15). Thomas is pale "with inward strife" (even after marrying Nell, he "gazed long" on Maude Clare, who is more **attractive** than Nell, by Nell's own admission- see lines 45-46); his mother, with joy; Nell, "with pride"; Maude Clare, presumably, with anger.

It is hard to ignore **an intertextual reference** here to the pale characters in Keats' ballad "La Belle Dame sans Merci", in which a knight allows himself to be seduced by a faery child; his

misplaced romantic obsession is a disaster, because it is so unrealistic, but he is not alone in experiencing the death of romance, and, with it, his own lingering decline- knights and kings before him have fallen for the same romantic illusion. Men, Keats says, are fatally prone to this. For Rossetti, it is perhaps **the only locus of power women have over men**, and the question becomes how women use it; responsibly or irresponsibly?

The focus in stanza 1 is on Maude Clare, who has witnessed the wedding ceremony (was she invited?) and walks with regal grandeur. The mother of the groom hopes that Thomas and Nell will "live true" for the next thirty years; in saying that her own husband "had just your tale to tell", she seems to concede that **men will have extra-marital relationships** before they settle down. Thomas' pallor indicates, however, that he is not over Maude Clare and that he has **doubts** over Nell- not a strong basis for the start of an exclusive relationship. He would in fact seem still to prefer to kiss Maude Clare if he had the choice (lines 15-16); in line 32, he cannot repudiate her, and he feels ashamed that he has rejected her.

The first four stanzas as a whole tell us that **all is not as it should be with this wedding**; there is a lack of frankness in Thomas and his mother. Stanzas 5 to 7 give Maude Clare the chance to vent her vengeful feelings of rejection. She sarcastically devalues the words "gift" and "bless" (and, by implication, devalues the new marriage), and uses **alliteration and repetition as an outlet for anger**. The apparent balance in the structure of stanzas 6 and 7 is really an emotional roadblock which she struggles to get past. The contrast she manages between what is budding now (lilies) and what has faded (leaves which were growing on the bough) is not altogether clear, because, to Victorians, lilies are symbols both of love and ardour, and (at funerals) of the return of the soul of the deceased to a state of innocence.

The emphasis in her final word in line 28- that the lilies may be budding *now* , but such romanticism will not last long- anticipates the potential for trouble which Nell's naïve optimism in the closing two stanzas hints at.

Having used stanzas 5-7 to attack Thomas, Maude Clare turns her attention to Nell in stanzas 9 and 10. Whereas Thomas was speechless, and unable to answer back, Nell delivers her own point of view in two stanzas of her own (11-12).

After presenting Thomas with "gifts" of half his gold chain and some dead leaves- the remains of their relationship- Maude Clare "gives" Nell not fruit or flowers (lines 35-36) but the half of Thomas' "fickle heart" which had supposedly been in her possession. The grandiose nature of this theatrical gesture is reflected in the rhetorical use of "thereof" to provide the rhyme in line 40- she would, in reality, say "I wash my hands of it".

Nell's response in the penultimate stanza is to **dress herself in the language of the marriage service** (take...for better and worse.... him I love), while in the final four lines she combines pragmatism- acknowledging that she is inferior to Maude Clare in height, wisdom and looks- with optimism. Nell believes that the enduring love she will direct at him will eventually be reciprocated. The narrator had told us as early as line 3 that Nell "was like a village maid"; this implies a lack of sophistication or worldliness in her expectations, but we do not know whether or not the narrator of this poem can be relied upon. Nell, unlike Thomas, does not have a mother present, to speak for her.

Who is the narrator of this poem? This is an interesting and largely unnoticed question. The narrator observes and records what is said and done outside the church- attributing body language and motivation to the dialogue, as a form of commentary on it. This narrator also refers to Thomas, in lines 13 and 15, as "My lord". Does this mean, in a final twist, that the narrator is now the wife of Thomas; that Nell, in asserting that he was her lord for better or worse (line 43) was to be disappointed, and that another woman has succeeded her? There is **another story here which the poem declines to tell.**

We are left with a richly dramatic poem which provokes us to think about **attitudes to marriage**; can it be approached idealistically and honestly or not? Can women rely on men, and can men rely on women? Where does the balance of power lie, and is that acceptable or desirable? Is the cultural supposition that marriage is permanent, exclusive and lifelong justified or indeed true? Do women rush into unsuitable marriages for material security or status, and do they know that being idealistic about the outcome will only lead to disappointment after the event?

The paleness of the bride and groom, Maude Clare and Thomas' mother extends the allusion to Keats' "La Belle Dame Sans Merci", to include **women as unintentional victims of the romantic delusion.** The gothic style which the poems share will tend to presuppose a tragic, rather than a happy, outcome. In Keats' poem, the knight **pursues the forbidden or unnatural**, and condemns himself to a long and lingering death; his romanticism is his own death warrant. There is nothing knightly about Thomas, but he may be labouring under the same misconception; **looking beyond what you have to what you cannot or should not have is a recipe for self-destruction.** A man whose heart lies elsewhere will not make a new wife happy. Is this, for Victorian women, the **unspoken reality of marriage**- the prelude to the bitter pair of poems which open your group?

We should note that the symbols in this poem could be understood as romantic markers of love- flowers, half of a golden chain, half a heart, and lilies. In Rossetti's poems, hearts are often literally broken (as we shall see in "Twice"). Half a heart and half a chain seek synthesis with their missing halves, but, once damaged, can they ever be repaired?

If we take the way symbols are used as a means of detecting meaning in a poem, the **negative application of the symbolic furniture** here is the opposite of those chosen to create the joyous mood in "A Birthday". Nothing there was faded or second-hand.

Uphill

The poem is in the simple form of a hymn, but it isn't a hymn. It sets out a series of questions and answers to those questions, like a canticle, or a **catechism**. While the length of the lines varies, there is a unifying rhyme scheme ABAB throughout. This creates **rigidity or reassuring certainty, depending on your point of view.**

Rossetti's poem "Amor Mundi" presents a walk on a downhill path as "easy.....hell's own track". In RL Stevenson's "Strange Case of Dr Jekyll and Mr Hyde", the lawyer Utterson has a philosophy of allowing fellow men to "go to the devil in his own way"; we are told that he was often "the last good influence in the lives of down-going men". The aphorism comes originally from Vergil's Aeneid- facilis descensus Averno- the descent to hell is easy.

It is therefore logical that the route to Heaven should be uphill. But **there is no mention of heaven** here. The poem is **devotional in character**, and it uses **religious language and euphemism** (a dark inn as **the graveyard**, our final **resting-place**, where we **fall asleep**; a long hard journey symbolising a long hard life). The trope of the journey describes and dramatizes the pilgrimage of the soul to death and........ to what? **Resurrection** in a Christian heaven? Or **just death**, just **lingering in a twilight zone** (as in "When I am dead, my dearest"?

Another very powerful poem of this type is Emily Dickinson's "Because I could not stop for death", which gives as journey's end "a House that seemed/A swelling of the ground"- the low mound of a grave. An elegiac poem about death- here, perhaps, death from physical or emotional exhaustion- does not have to be redemptive.

The lexical representation of life is in the words and phrases "road/ end/day's journey/ the whole long day/ morn to night"; at the end of life, we are "sore and weak".

Euphemisms for death are "the very end/night/ to night/ for the night/ a resting-place/ the slow dark hours/ the darkness/ at night/ door/beds". The dead are "those who have gone before"- the uphill journey is not resumed after a night's rest. **Night, dark and darkness dominate** the poem.

The use of euphemism normalises the thoughts of death, but this inn is unusual in that it offers an infinite number of beds, in that nobody is turned away; **the ranks of the dead are never full. It is impossible to "miss that inn" because we will all die.** Tellingly, death is presented in stanza 3 as a private event; it is not conducted in the presence of "other wayfarers", but is a process of following "those who have gone before".

If the person asking the questions is the narrator, **the other responding speaker is presumably death or God or a priest who conducts funerals. Their character is authoritative and slightly sinister.** They offer no opt-out.

Life is presented here as laborious and tiring; rest comes only at its end at night, in the form of oblivion.

It is hardly an inspiring message, this- that life is tough, and then you die, alone, without the promise of anything beyond death. There is no resurrection or salvation here.

Death is not contextualised here; **it is a stand-alone event** which does not appear to lead anywhere else. With the symbolism of the inn and the journey, and the choice of presenting life as laborious and exhausting, the poem feels as though it takes us back to an earlier age- if not of feudalism, then at least to Blake, and his twin concerns- morality and organised religion, and industrialisation.

Obliquely, this poem could be a social commentary on the plight of the labouring class, and a challenge to the established Church as the provider of insight and consolation. The narrator asks a series of eight questions, which take up all the odd lines of the poem.

The answers are comforting and not comforting at the same time. This question/answer formula is like a church canticle- an article of faith which no one is allowed to disbelieve in.

The poem seems also to be **sceptical about a benevolent God**. The question of why a good God would allow so much suffering is an age-old one. The poem seems to **doubt whether we get our reward for a hard-working diligent life in the afterlife; we're dead. Dying is** when "the slow dark hours begin"- the "very end" of a long uphill journey, but **not the beginning of something else.**

The dead are undead, and lacking comfort, in others of Rossetti's poems. In "At Home", the narrator, a ghost, is acutely conscious that the simple pleasures of life on earth are no longer accessible. In "The Poor Ghost", the living choose to continue to live; love of the recently dead is not a strong enough bond to motivate you to join them, and so the ghost must lie in a grave till Judgement Day.

The narrators in these two Rossetti poems had enjoyed, it seems, a companionable and civilised life, with relaxation and company at its heart; a (premature) death is therefore a deprivation and a sacrifice, when death is seen in a secular context.

In "Uphill", the questioner seems to hope that death is **a peaceful and restful end to struggle**; but the answerer offers no prospect of a peace which can be enjoyed, but only the prospect of oblivion- **an enforced lack of activity**.

The questions are always couched in lines of ten syllables, with the single exception of nine in line 1. The answers are shorter- five of them only have six syllables. It is as if **there is a refusal to elaborate or to engage in discussion, on the part of the death figure.**

What are we to make of this refusal to offer the hope of anything to console you after death? Life after death seems, in the world of this poem, to have nothing to recommend it.

It is conceivable that the poem offers an argument that there is a faith-sized hole in our lives; that without Christian belief in life after death, life loses meaning. If this is the point of "Uphill" it is hard to detect it.

It is more productive to read this poem in the light of the shadowless spirit, the gatekeeper in "Shut Out". **No-one will give us answers to the existentialist need we have to make sense of our own existence.** The established church may not be very good at making its messages about death seem convincing, but ultimately we have to decide for ourselves what our life means and what it is important to do with it.

Finally, a word about intertextuality. The addressing of the travelling soul as a friend, the many rooms in the inn and the idea of knocking on the door (of heaven?) leads some readers to jump to the conclusion that this is a New Testament- inspired poem, where salvation lies somewhere in the darkness (not, you will note, in the poem itself). In particular, St John 14:2- "In my Father's house are many mansions.....I go to prepare a place for you" - has led some commentators to think that the respondent is Christ, and that the travelling soul has nothing to worry about.

We have seen that, in Maude Clare, Nell quotes from the marriage service; the fact that she does cannot be taken as a sign, for instance, that her own marriage will be a success. The lexical field of death is stronger than the lexical field of the Gospels in "Uphill", and there is a deliberate vagueness or complexity about the identity of the persona who delivers the answers to the questions, which renders the association of the inn with Heaven trite.

Rossetti's religious belief will not have made her immune to seeing faults in the Church. In fact, she will have seen such an arch-patriarchal institution as prone to accentuating the faults of the male psyche. There is no inconsistency between her poems which catch a religious confidence and engage with the Christian concept of Heaven, and the ones which express a doubtful instinct. The Church asks and requires you to believe in its goblin fruit, but there is no guarantee that its appearance reflects its substance. Perhaps the Christian promise of salvation is like Rossetti's secrets; known to itself, or hinted at, or really something which does not exist, because there is no secret at all.

"No, Thank You, John"

This poem is at least **partly autobiographical**; Rossetti rejected a proposal by the portrait painter John Brett in the 1850s. According to her brother she made a pencil note that he was "obnoxious" because he would not take a polite no for an answer. In most of the group of poems you are studying, there is **an aesthetic dimension**. "A Birthday" creates a rarefied pictorial beauty, and emotional intensity is captured and held up for us, also, in "Shut Out", "Echo" and "In the Round Tower at Jhansi", for example. Rossetti often **creates contexts in which her characters have no option but to confront intense emotion.** These contexts are often **religious or matrimonial**, and they can involve physical danger or- more usually- grief, longing, regret or uncertainty.

This quality is absent in **this poem**, which **satirises or trivialises misdirected feeling on the part of the addressee.** In **considering the issue of marriage, Rossetti's poems usually examine imbalances of power,** which are (during the lifetime of the marriage) in favour of the male, because Victorian marriage is so patriarchal. **Here, the power to decide, the power of speech, and the power to say no all belong to the female character** who is the object of pursuit; **an inversion of the traditional** pattern. Just as "Remember" is an inversion of the sonnet- it is a poem of resentment and hatred, not of love- and just as the central role of the pale young wife at Jhansi, and the pale women in Maude Clare who take the centre of the stage are inversions of the expectations of masculine and feminine behaviour, here we have **a female narrator speaking with a**

blunt directness and a lack of empathy which we would see as masculine in character.

At the same time, the subtext which runs here and through the poems of female exclusion and frustration too, coexists with this confounding of the norm- the idea that **women must resist the temptation to undervalue themselves.** This theme finds its most explicit expression, among the set poems, in Goblin Market.

The form- eight quatrains with an ABAB rhyme scheme- generates **a grim lightness and momentum in this monologue.** All the stanzas are end-stopped until the end of stanza 7; the narrator's impatience cannot, by then, be contained any longer and it spills over the constraint of the end of the stanza.

The structure of the poem falls into two halves. Lines 1-15 set out the narrator's position, with a **wide range of sentence structures and punctuation (including three questions) to create the impression that John is slow on the uptake and reluctant to face facts.** Then, from line 16 to the end of the poem, there is **the familiar list of injunctions or imperatives-** use/let/don't/ let's/catch/forget/ let/ don't/ rise- as a combination of impatience and compassion aims to redirect John's energies into more productive and less tiresome behaviour.

The poem comprises eight sentences, all of which are variations on the mission of delivering a rejection. It is done without any sentimentality. When Jessie Cameron does the same in the poem named after her, she too lists the names of other women who might be "good" for the defective suitor. That poem is a ballad, which turns into a tragedy of black magic and revenge. Here, Rossetti aims to apply a humorous approach to a one-sided infatuation. To modern tastes, Victorian humour can often feel heavy-handed and a little relentless; if we find that impulse here, it will be because the poem could be shorter- the "joke" perhaps goes on too long. In this context, stanza 2 is almost an exact restatement of stanza 1, in an identical form.

Evidently John has been so slow to accept the narrator's rejection of him that this extended and unambiguous declamation is justified. The questions in the first three stanzas indicate what he has said to her- "Do please marry me; do please say yes; I am pining for you; If you won't marry me I will be single for ever; you are false and you misled me; don't withhold your affection by being cruel and heartless". These attitudes are all, in the narrator's mind, sentimental rubbish; she protests that she has never given him any indication that she intended to be more than a friend.

The poem is assembled from a combination of iambic pentameters, tetrameters and trimeters. **The last line of the**

poem, with only 4 syllables, is an emphatic and exasperated closure. Stanzas 1, 2, 3, 6 and 7 all follow an identical pattern of syllables per line (8/8/10/6) and there is only slight variation of this in stanzas 4 (9/8/10/6) and 8 (8/8/10/4); **stanza 5** disrupts the pattern (6/10/10/6) and it is the bluntest passage; **the electric shock** which the narrator hopes will jolt him out of his complacency.

The negatives begin to pile up in the middle part of the poem- no/not/don't/not/ not/no / no dominate lines 13- 22, whereas the opening and close of the poem deals in opposites (never/always, off and on).

Perhaps the poem intends to use its humorous tone to make a more serious point; that women should be unafraid to reject unsuitable men or unsuitable proposals; there is no harm in saying "no" and holding out for a better offer. **The inversion of the speaking voices makes the point that women have thoughts and voices of their own, and that they are often more logical, clear-headed and right than men.** This is a different way of making the same point as in "Maude Clare", where Thomas is voiceless. "From the Antique" gives a voice to women's sense that they are denied a voice.

All of **these poems give the lie to the truism that "men think, but women feel"; women are just as capable as men, if not better, at making discriminating judgments.** As a group, these poems present women as more patient and long-suffering than men, and **more capable of absorbing disappointment; more loyal; just as brave** (Mrs Skene). They are also oppressed and abused, emotionally and sometimes physically, and their opportunities to determine their own destinies are too few ("Shut Out"). Generally, the poems warn women not to compromise, where accepting second best leaves them vulnerable to damage. Nell may be as wrong about Thomas as John is here about the narrator of this poem, but why should women not exercise the same freedoms of choice as men?

Good Friday

This is an **aesthetic** and a **religious** poem, in which the narrator berates and laments her lack of capacity to feel the raw grief at the Crucifixion which some of those who were there are recorded as feeling.

The contrast between the narrator, and those she compares herself with unfavourably, is generated by the use of a rhetorical question which forms the opening stanza, contrasted with the four repeated "not so"s in lines 5-9.

Rather like "A Birthday", which also deals with the emotions of religious devotion, this is a **highly pictorial** poem; we can imagine the narrator standing at the scene of the Crucifixion (although this is an anomaly because she could not be present at an event two millennia earlier!), as her focus moves from the bleeding to the various witnesses in stanza two and then the darkness of the eclipse in stanza 3.

The poem is **an imaginative extension of the very brief accounts of the Crucifixion in the four gospels**; the personification of the sun and the moon in the third stanza is a literary touch, but we can visualise it, too, as a feature in some imaginary medieval painting of the scene.

The form of the poem- four quatrains with an ABBA rhyme scheme in stanzas 1 and 2, then ABAB for stanzas 3 and 4- uses variety in the lengths of lines and the syllable count, to reflect the contrast between the confident analysis in the inner two lines of each stanza, each of which has ten syllables, and the **inadequacy** the narrator feels, in terms of the poverty of her own response; the outer lines in stanzas 1 and 2 have a total of 12 syllables (8 and 4, 6 and 6), and stanzas 3 and 4 have 10 then 8 (6 and 4, 4 and 4). Where the form of a poem allows it, Rossetti prefers to use words more economically in the final line of a poem; she perceives it as a way of reaching a true conclusion.

Just as in "Maude Clare", where **the focus shifts to the higher-minded Nell in the final lines, here the closing stanza moves away from the narrator to Christ,** whom she calls upon- in the form of an imprecation or prayer- to provide a transforming moment in which her capacity for grief will be released at a stroke.

The repetition of "sheep" (lines 1 and 14) and the similarity of "stone" in line 1 and "rock" in line 16 gives the poem thematic unity. We talk of the difficulty of getting blood out of a stone; the poem contrasts the hard materials with blood and tears.

Religious poems are by nature contemplative rather than narrative; Rossetti's response here, as in the second half of "A Birthday", is to paint a word picture, using the language and diction of the Bible.

Twice

It is possible to argue that the explanation for why there is no Heaven in "Up-hill" and no language to grieve what, to a Christian, is the most grievous event of all in "Good Friday" is that the language of superlatives and of the most intensity has lost its power and resonance because of its application to (less transcendent) human romantic relationships.

In "Twice", **Rossetti explores whether you can use the language of romantic love to express the devotional intensity she sought in "Good Friday";** the poem also reflects her own life experience of declining to marry and transferring her romantic energy to God as a better and more reliable patriarchal model!

The six octaves of "Twice" have a rhyme scheme ABACDBDC, apart from **one significant exception-** the second half of stanza 4 (ABACABAD), where **the protest against the dysfunctionality of relationships with men is at its loudest**, and turns to God instead.

The rhyme scheme is **extremely restrictive**; it reflects the narrator's **desperate feeling of voicelessness** (But this once hear me speak, line 5). We have seen in other poems Rossetti's tendency to abbreviate the length of the line as a poem develops, and she does that here; in the last twenty lines, the average number of syllables per line is six, and there are only three seven-syllable lines, compared with twelve in the first twenty-eight lines.

The structure of the poem also reflects structures we have met before- after **an exposition** which brings us to the present moment, and is **narrated in the past tense**, in the first three stanzas, the **second half of the poem moves into the present tense and unleashes a series of imperatives** which the narrator implores God to act upon- judge/take/refine/purge/hold/smile. The closing stanza **yokes together the language of the Last Judgment and the language of the marriage service** (lines 45-46).

The title of the poem implies that there will be repetition within it. In fact there is relatively little repetition of words (heart x 6, hand x 5) apart from the pronouns I me, my, you and your, Thou and Thy. **The repetition is rather in the action**-of having your heart examined by a man who judges it immature and unripe and by God, who, you hope, will find it imperfect but perfectible.

The refrain "O my love" in lines 2 and 6 is **reshaped** the second time as "O my God" (lines 26 and 30); "your judgment" in line 20 becomes "Thy judgment" in line 31. Unlike the human patriarch, who rejects the narrator's heart in stanza 2, God does not speak.

Stanza 1 sets out the framework of the poem- it is motivated by the need to be allowed to speak, just for once (line 5). Yet the narrator yields immediately to the notion that the man should speak- and the result is that her heart is broken, on the grounds that it is "unripe" (lacking in wisdom). **The extended metaphor of the broken heart conveys the idea that a relationship in which the female partner is patronised and denied a voice cannot work.** In the human dimension, all she can do is smile and accept the judgment (that she is immature and has nothing worthwhile to say) but this is a path to the narrator's personal misery and disengagement (stanza 3).

Following that scornful and dismissive human judgment, standing "contemned of a man" (line 35), the narrator presents her (now broken) heart for judgment again in stanza 4. Stanza 5 explains that the narrator wants her heart to be damaged no more than it has been already; she wants to hand it to God for protection and safe keeping (and to be purified).

In the final stanza, the narrator says that God has called her (to eternal life) and that **she is summoned to marry him. Unlike the smile of the human suitor (line 10), which rejected her and put an end to the narrator's singing or joy (line 24), God's smile (line 47) will prompt the narrator to sing** again. The unfavourable verdict of her human judge left her so crushed that she did not question it (line 22), but accepted it passively;

whatever God's judgment (which is left beyond the end of the poem, but which we know will be accepting) she will have the option to challenge it, even if she chooses not to question it "much" (line 48). The difference is that your relationship with an all-seeing God is penetrating, but progressive. God can "scan" your heart, "refine" it and keep it safe ("hold it"). Your human judge simply sends you away, to seek greater wisdom, but that is impossible when you have **no voice and no possibility of development**.

Like the gatekeeper in "Shut Out", the man in this poem excludes the narrator from her aspiration, casually if not cruelly. In "Maude Clare", there were two women and a man deciding between them, and in "No, thank you, John" there was a rejected man. Here, we have **a rejected woman, and God in place of Nell, as the constant, morally improving, superhuman source of a love superior to day-to-day human love** in ordinary male-female relationships. There is a sense in "Twice" that the powerful love of God is a second choice; it only becomes desirable in the absence of a workable relationship with a human lover. However, God will not disappoint you with the kind of casual character assassination and dismissal of your potential we find in stanzas 2 and 3.

The purging from sin, in order to improve her heart, which the narrator volunteers to undergo in stanza 5, is provoked by her earlier rejection. Renouncing sin and embracing the religious life, whether or not this is prompted by being tired of the treatment men mete out, prompts "Soeur Louise de la Misericorde" too.

While "Twice" does manage to convey **the emotional white heat of religious belief** (the intensity which is elusive in "Good Friday")- by virtue of the **imagery of fire, gold, and refining**, its deeper purpose may well be to offer, in those key stanzas 2 and 3, a critique of how and why Victorian marriage tends not to work- because of how women then had no voice.

Goblin Market

This is a complex and very long poem; it has **elements of the fairy tale, the horror story, Biblical/Christian undertones of temptation/sin/redemption/sacrifice/ Garden of Eden, and a subtext about female desire- all these themes are brought together in the phrase "the fruit forbidden".** Because of the length and importance of this poem, I have divided my study of it into sections in this guide.

Plot summary

Laura's **curiosity** about the goblins, and the exotic fruit they sell, **overcomes** her proper sense of **"restraint".** She has no money, but she has a "sweet tooth"; she gives the goblins a lock of her hair and then has an orgiastic binge with their fruit.

Lizzie tells Laura off, and reminds her that Jeanie had pined away and died when she became obsessed with the goblins.

The next day, Laura is in "an absent dream.....longing for the night....like a leaping flame". The goblins do not reappear; Laura ages and is discontented and distressed, because she cannot hear the goblins' cry of temptation; she cannot repeat the experience of intense pleasure.

Lizzie, however, can hear the goblins, and, because Laura has stopped eating, she wants to buy the fruit, not for her own pleasure, but to save Laura. She takes a silver penny and allows the goblins to put on their elaborate performance in front of her. They hug/kiss/ squeeze/ caress her; she refuses to stay for their feast, but simply wants to take the fruit she buys back to Laura. The goblins become abusive, intimidating and violent, and they "squeezed their fruits / Against her mouth to make her eat". A sequence of five similes emphasises Lizzie's **heroism**. She holds out against the bullying, scratching and pinching of the "evil people". The goblins throw her coin back, and disappear, both over and underground.

When Laura kisses Lizzie's fruit-stained face, she is cured; the spell or curse is broken in a kind of **involuntary exorcism**, described in nine more similes. The lesson is learnt, and passed on to their own children; that sisters protect each other from harm.

Themes and context

Rossetti's brother William (whose testimony is not always entirely reliable) said that she did not mean the poem to say anything "profound" and that it is a "fairy tale", not a morality tale.

The symbolism- especially to do with the fruit and the goblins- is graphic and powerful; the poem ends like a medieval romance.

Laura and Lizzie are so close that they are almost the same- two aspects of a single personality. Their uneasy task is to reconcile **the desire to be conventional**- to look after the cottage, and keep out of trouble- **and the desire to give in to the temptation** the (male) goblins bring to a chaste and sterile female environment.

There are some interesting parallels with Stevenson's (as yet unwritten) tale of Jekyll and Hyde; Jekyll is a respectable citizen but he is curious about forbidden scientific knowledge and about the duality of his own personality. He unleashes Hyde, with unintended consequences. The story is a gothic morality tale, but, on a deeper level, it raises the ethical question of the boundaries of knowledge and **whether we should be punished for being curious. Rossetti's protagonists are children, who hover on the margins of the dangers of prostitution, just as Jekyll hovers on the margins of experimental chemistry. The world of the unknown and the surreal disrupts and makes us wiser, in both stories.**

Rossetti's own refusal to marry is reflected, at some level, in the suppression and extinguishing of the power of temptation in the poem. She had broken off her engagement to James Collinson in 1847 and she declined a marriage proposal from Charles Cayley in the 1860s. "Goblin Market" was published in 1862.

The engagement with the goblins is a clash of good v evil and male v female. The two girls are depicted as strong and sympathetic personalities, but they are vulnerable to the goblins' curse and their violence. **The goblins are sexual predators**. Do they symbolise men? All men? Some men?

"Goblin Market" moves **from dissatisfaction to satisfaction** (in motherhood), unlike most of the other poems, which end with the same dissatisfaction and unhappiness (in wifehood) they started with.

We have (in Laura, and the dead girl Jeanie) the **obsessive** tendency, but it is balanced by Lizzie's **strength and resilience in the face of a sexual assault**.

You will need to decide what the themes are (feminism, male dominance and power, religious morality etc) and put them in some **hierarchy of importance**. I would call the poem **a fairy tale for adults, because it has a dark side,** created by the energy of the symbolism. It varies in its style and tone, in ways which don't arise in the shorter poems. The narrative voice here is not necessarily a woman's, but female behaviour is evaluated in an apparently objective way by a narrator who is sympathetic to Lizzie and Laura.

Explorations of **context** here are very varied. From the **autobiographical perspective**, Rossetti's work with, and compassion for, "fallen women" sheds some light on the economic vulnerability of the sisters and on the characterisation of the goblins as **predatory males who want (domestic) control-** they only want girls who will sit down and eat with them.

The Spring of 1859- when the poem was completed- brought extremes of weather which decimated domestic fruit crops. There was already a taste for importing fruit, and for developing more intensive propagation methods to meet a growing consumer demand, especially from the expanding middle class. The goblins' fruit is of unproveable provenance (and dubious quality) and there is a sense that it robs its victims of their identity. It is **impure**, and consuming it **infects** the consumer with a wasting disease. Perhaps there is a coded message here about the dangers of colonialism, in the sense that mixed marriage somehow dilutes or weakens the national identity. Colonists might **import** new strains of infectious disease (bring it home or take it abroad) - there is a subtext here about Britain's international economic expansion in the mid-nineteenth century (and now we have Brexit, and endless speculation about global trading- again!).

The description of Jeanie has connotations of **prostitution**- rather like the young harlot in Blake's "London". **The goblins have no interest in selling fruit to married women**- in fact, they receive no money from the sisters at all; **they are pimps of fruit who may well seek simply to trap young girls into prostitution.** The sisters are of an indeterminate age, but, as "maids", if they are at the age of consent- which was only 12- they would be prey for prostitution, if they did not have the means to support themselves on their farm.

Feminist critics will argue that the poem dramatises the economic poverty of (unmarried) women; all they have to

bargain with is their bodies, or, more precisely, perhaps, their **virginity**. The sisters are sexually curious, but premarital sex (Jeanie) is presented as fatal.

One of the **more imaginative critical approaches to the tale is that "Lizzie" is the established poet Elizabeth Barrett Browning, and "Laura" is Rossetti** herself, striving to establish her own place in literary history and to become worthy of the challenge of succeeding her as the poetic voice of Victorian women.

A Freudian analysis might link the dream-like and surreal aspects of the poem with sexual fantasies of various kinds. Readers who engage with Jan Morris' hypothesis that Rossetti was sexually abused by her father, and that this provoked her illnesses (Anaemia? Depression?) and withdrawal, **will find plenty of circumstantial evidence here.**

My personal view is that we should look in the text for clues. The world of the poem is binary- **men are dynamic "doers", with an animal energy and no moral responsibility.** They pursue power and wealth and they operate in male networks.

Women, from adolescence, are expected to be domesticised, modest, uneducated homebodies with simple tastes. Outside the home, they may be victims of men's sexual violence, and then outcast. Laura's single slip into temptation and consuming the forbidden fruit is not fatal; Jeanie dies because she had no sister to save her. Lizzie's saving sexual humiliation rehabilitates Laura; the poem seems to be saying that **female sexuality should not be judged by men** because they exploit it and do not understand it.

Perhaps the choice of the name "Laura" is significant. Laura is the insubstantial and romanticised (Italian) love object in Petrarch's sonnets; Christina Rossetti's version of Laura is only too willing to expose herself to contact with the goblins.

The **theme of renunciation**- of giving up normal human pleasures and pursuing a more sanctified life in which God features prominently- runs through Rossetti's poems. **Specifically, it is the aesthetic pleasure of the finer things of life which is renounced,** and **the fruit here is not desired as a way of satisfying hunger**, but for its texture, its flavour, its exotic, global foreignness and the fact that it is forbidden because it is bad for maids. **Sexual experience and knowledge before marriage reduces the value of girls in the marriage market** and opens them to shame. If Rossetti herself found it impossible to accept marriage proposals because she felt defiled after experiencing sexual abuse herself, as an adolescent, her own odd claim that the poem is merely to be read as a nursery story would be more explicable. This also establishes a link with the idea of secrets, and keeping them. **Is there an autobiographical**

secret here? Are Laura and Lizzie in fact Christina and her sister Maria?

Commentary

The poem opens with a repetition of the goblins' cry- as though the first version is the one in the morning and the second the one in the evening, while the hawking cry is also in the form of a continuous loop. They include the urgent refrains "come buy…taste them and try". Some of the fruits are native to the UK and others (dates) have to be imported. This opening is **aural, not visual**. Lines 5-31 list 29 different products, accompanied by adjectives which emphasise their quality and naturalness.

It is **only "maids"** who **can hear the siren song of the goblins-** experienced women cannot. The closing lines of the poem make it clear that the fruit is a deception- "like honey to the throat/ But poison in the blood"; and, significantly, real markets in real towns do not sell these fruits- they are more imagined than real.

Of the two alliterative sisters, crouching closely in the cooling evening, Laura listens to the call intently, but she thinks she can resist temptation; she tells Lizzie that they must not look at the goblins or buy their produce because

Who knows upon what soil they fed

Their hungry thirsty roots?

This is the language of obsession and enchantment (reminiscent of Keats' "La Belle Dame sans Merci"). Lizzie covers her eyes (covered close lest they should look), but Laura, "pricking up her golden head....reared her glossy head", describes the sight of the goblins- their dishes and their appearance (not the fruit, because we have already been told what is on the menu). Lizzie refuses Laura's command to look, maintaining that "their evil gifts would harm us". We understand that the two maids must present a united front- divided, they will fall.

Lizzie- childishly but wisely- sticks her fingers in her ears, shuts her eyes and runs away, while "curious Laura" continues to gaze at the goblins, and describes them in animal, subhuman terms- cats, rats, snails and wombats all lack nobility but they are not dangerous to humans.

When the goblins speak, **Laura hears their voices "like voice of doves/Cooing all together", which is either a deception or a misjudgement. When Lizzie visits them later, they chatter like magpies and flutter like pigeons; they have harmed Laura and their romantic aura has gone.**

The narrator intervenes, to direct the reader, with a series of four similes, in which we are told that the swan-like Laura inclines towards the goblins like a ship whose momentum is headlong –

Like a vessel at the launch

When its **last restraint is gone**.

There is therefore no intention to keep the reader guessing- **no dramatic tension**. The goblins repeat their "come buy" injunction- it is **a "shrill repeated cry", not a cooing of doves**. A brief and awkward presentation by the goblins follows. They have a well-rehearsed routine, which includes one goblin weaving a crown out of tendrils, leaves and nuts- an artefact which, once more, is **not for sale by men in any town.**

The narrator tells us, in the middle of a description which moves from choreography to a chorus of voices, that Laura "longed but had no money". She "stared but did not stir"- it is a scene reminiscent of a rugby team watching the New Zealand All Blacks' haka, a sinister dance of welcome and challenge. The goblins here are "queer" and "sly"- **they want to destroy Laura.**

Then Laura speaks for herself, "in haste", ceding the initiative to the goblins by admitting the weakness of her position- her money is far away, at home. The goblins will, instead, accept "a golden curl" of her hair, which she gives them ("she clipped a precious golden lock"); is this a reversal of Samson and Delilah? She lets a tear fall as she hands over her hair- it is, on some level, **a yielding of power, a trophy,** a notch on some man's bedpost. A surrender of innocence; it could be produced as evidence of her betrayal of the innocence of the maid.

Laura then tastes the fruit (like Eve in the Garden of Eden); it is described in comparative adjectives, "sweeter….stronger….clearer", and a rhetorical question stresses its attraction. The word "sucked" is used five times, culminating in the line **"she sucked until her lips were sore"**. She goes home with "one kernel-stone"- presumably, to grow her own fruit, but it will not germinate, because the goblins' fruit is artificial. There is no chewing here, **no solid substance to the fruit**. It is described purely in terms of **liquids- honey, wine, water, juice. This, and the emphasis on sucking, implies , not thirst, but novelty ("she never tasted such before")**; the knowledge of Adam and Eve, translated into mid-nineteenth century England and its acceptance of prostitution, becomes, more narrowly, the technique of fellatio.

Lizzie is waiting for her at the gate, and she repeats her "wise upbraidings", unaware of what Laura has done. Now we have **the terrible gothic melodrama of Jeanie, who did precisely what Laura has just done, and then faded away, died, and is buried in barren or accursed ground no flowers grow on.** This, again, is reminiscent, though with a gender reversal, of the knight in Keats' poem- seduced by an evil spirit and condemned to die for leaving the orthodox path he should have followed. Romantic curiosity and passion is suicidal. Jeanie had tried to find the goblins, but, after initiating her into the world of heterosexual sex, they were finished with her, because her maidenhood was no longer a currency she could trade with.

Laura confesses that she, like Jeanie, is under the compulsive spell of the fruit, and she promises to bring fruit for Lizzie tomorrow. She describes the **tastes and textures** of the fruits she has tried in **sensuous** terms. They then sleep "in their curtained bed", with a list of four similes emphasising that they are effectively a single entity- the fate of one will be the fate of both. Lizzie has not told Laura not to return to the goblins the next night- knowing that, as with Jeanie, they will not be found, because they are no longer accessible to her- but she seems not to fear, yet, that Laura will now dwindle and die.

The description of their routine the next morning combines the harmless and domestic with the "warning" of the first cock crow (a reference to St Matthew's Gospel). Lizzie's "open heart…..content….placid" and sexless, contrasts with Laura's desperate "longing for the night"- the forbidden, the occult, the male.

The phrase "slow evening" here, like "man-rejoicing wine" earlier, may strike you as ominous. You will also notice **the piling up of similes at moments of heroism or crisis** later in this poem.

These language features are a nod in the direction of the Greek epic poet Homer, to whom authorship of the Iliad and the Odyssey is ascribed. Indeed, the goblins' "siren song" is reminiscent of book 12 of the Odyssey and the story of the Sirens.

 As it gets dark, we remember that Lizzie has already pronounced that "Twilight is not good for maidens"; Laura refuses to go home, hoping to hear the goblins' call, "with its iterated jingle/ of sugar-baited words". Lizzie hears "the fruit-call" and urges Laura to go home with her before nightfall, in case they get lost in a midsummer storm.

Her advice falls on deaf ears; **the example of the tragic Jeanie leaves the reader well aware, in advance, that addiction or compulsion will always trump quiet propriety.** Unless she is keeping a secret (from her own life) from us, **Christina Rossetti, the unfallen woman, understands why the fallen or betrayed woman is so seduced; perhaps she has, albeit mistakenly, felt significant or powerful for the only time in her life.**

Laura is distraught that she herself cannot hear the cry of the goblins, so that she cannot experience the sensuous rush again, but has, in effect, become "deaf and blind"; she "trudged home", and sits up after Lizzie has fallen asleep, "in a passionate yearning......baulked desire". The description here is Chaucerian, and it seems slightly ironic.

Days and nights pass, but Laura, in her "exceeding pain", cannot see or hear the goblins. She (like Jeanie before her) starts to be ill- "her hair grew thin and grey", where it had been golden and glossy before. **The reader will feel that her death is inevitable; she has made the same error as Jeanie and her fate will be the same.**

She tries to make "her kernel-stone" grow in the sun but it will not yield any fruit. Now she has "sunk eyes and faded mouth" as if she is a traveller in the desert, tormented by an optical illusion of an oasis. **The language is now of thirst** (moisture/ false waves/ drouth/ thirstier). **An aesthetic thirst for forbidden knowledge has given way to a physical thirst** she cannot satisfy. The extended four-line simile here is mock-epic; it hints at a serious predicament but also holds out the prospect of some solution. Meanwhile she lapses into a state of listless myopia (ME?) characterised by one of Rossetti's familiar "no" lists- a list of what she does not do.

Lizzie still hears the goblins; she wants to help Laura, but the plot is weak here; why should she supply drugs to her dependent sister? She apparently wants to "share" "her sister's cankerous care"- this implies she has the same gothic death wish. Uncorrupted, and therefore able to hear the goblins, her dilemma is presented as follows-   she

Longed to buy fruit to comfort her,

But feared to pay too dear.

She reflects on the fate of Jeanie, who had died in her prime "for joys brides hope to have"; this means **she had died as a punishment for the sin of sex before marriage.** It is as though Lizzie recognises that Laura is under a death sentence, but she wants to fetch her more fruit as a source of consolation to her dying sister. Only the fact that **Laura's death seems imminent** stops Lizzie's worries about the price; she goes to buy the fruit, armed with "a silver penny", and she looks out for the goblins on her own account. **As a maid, she is treated to the full display, and more- she is "hugged…. kissed…… squeezed and caressed".**

The goblins, surprisingly perhaps, are not interested in a commercial transaction. Instead, they want to **humiliate** Lizzie. They want her to sit down and eat with them (a perversion of the Last Supper); they point out that taking the fruit away would compromise its flavour (no doubt they want to **see it sucked** as Laura had sucked it- till "her lips were sore").

When Lizzie ("mindful of Jeanie") refuses to accept their so-called hospitality, saying that she wants to buy fruit, but only if she can take it away, they become aggressive, "grunting….snarling"; they jostle her, elbow her, tread on her, claw at her clothes, pull her hair out "by the roots" (an echo of the roots of the goblins' fruit-trees?), stamp on her feet, and, most shockingly,

Held her hands and squeezed their fruits

Against her mouth to make her eat.

This is sexually penetrative and coercive, although Victorian Law did not protect prostitutes effectively against sexual violence. The goblins simply seek sexual and physical power over Lizzie. **The allegory here may be that even bringing assets of your own into a (commercial) marriage is no guarantee of humane treatment for a "maid".**

The goblins' speech is a chorus of "barking, mewing, hissing, mocking". This description evokes the scourging of Christ before the crucifixion, and perhaps the public mocking of criminals who are to be executed in public in Victorian England. In the light of possible interpretations of other poems of Rossetti's – if you believe they are a commentary on male/domestic violence and the abuse of women- you need to consider the feminist undertones here.

The threat of force feeding is left hanging while the narrator takes **a 16-line detour with a cluster of five similes,** which describe Lizzie in the heroic manner, and in **the tradition of the virtuous woman** which goes back to Chaucer and even earlier in Roman/Latin literature. The virtuous woman, faced with a dilemma in which she is sexually compromised, chooses to lose her life rather than her honour- there is something of this, too, in Juliet's attempts to avoid a bigamous marriage to Paris in Act 4 of Shakespeare's "Romeo and Juliet".

These similes about Lizzie convey a sense of baiting a helpless victim- through nature, in floods and storms at sea, and predatory wasps and bees- and then, "like a royal virgin town" with golden domes (like the golden Lizzie) besieged by a hostile fleet (like the goblin "merchant" transport)-

Mad to drag her standard down.

Lizzie remains calm, statuesque, unresponsive; but, inwardly, she is laughing, because she knows she has won the battle through passive resistance. The battle is the conflict between maidenly propriety and the forbidden fruit.

It is clear that the goblins want to use their fruit to destroy "maidens" by coercing them into eating it- like the serpent with Eve, in the Garden of Eden. Rossetti will have known Milton's epic poem "Paradise Lost", and the goblins "writhed into the ground" and otherwise vanished, rather as a Miltonic serpent might, when they are defeated by her resistance.

After these similes, the goblins' physical assault continues, but it seems less intense, because we know now that they will not succeed. Lizzie seems to have little trouble keeping her mouth shut "lest they should cram a mouthful in", while she "laughed in heart" as the juices run down her face and neck.

The bullying goblins finally lose interest, because of her defiance, her principled resistance. **Although she has not eaten the fruit, the effect of her experience is the same as it was for Laura- she**

Knew not was it night or day

- exactly the same form of words had applied to her sister early in the poem. It is not Lizzie's mouth which is sore, though- she has been punched, kicked and bruised all over.

Keeping her money is "music to her ear"; for Lizzie, facing the goblins down is a personal triumph and a solution for Laura, because it has broken their spell. Her "inward laughter" reflects a quiet moral triumph over "evil".

She tells Laura to

Hug me, kiss me, suck my juices

Squeezed from goblin fruits for you

and **the line "Eat me, drink me, love me" is an echo of the Communion service.** Lizzie had been worried that she would have to pay too high a price to save her sister from the goblins, but all she has suffered is some scratching and "bruises"; she had her money back. She tells Laura specifically that she has

"braved the glen/ And had to do with goblin merchant men"
"for your sake"; **consorting with evil, as a maiden, is rather like the submission and the redemptive self-sacrifice of Christ, as well as tasting "the fruit forbidden".**

Laura thinks that Lizzie has really eaten the fruit, and so condemned herself to the same wasting death that Jeanie suffered and which she anticipates for herself. Her kisses are of appreciation and empathy and admiration, but the fruit-stains on Lizzie's face are the antidote- because they have been won without being shamed.

A type of exorcism takes place, accompanied by nine more similes; this evokes the description in Keats' poem "Lamia" of the metamorphosis of Lamia from a snake to a woman. The exorcism is a dramatic process which ends with a rhetorical question- is Laura dead or alive?

Shakespeare's Othello accuses his wife (Desdemona) of harbouring a "sweating devil"- her so-called sins- which needs to be exorcised. The fire which now sweeps through Laura overcomes the (lesser) fire of sin/evil the goblins had afflicted her with; **the goblins' curse is extinguished by a form of death and resurrection ("Life out of death").**

By the next morning, Laura is restored to her former "innocent" self, and her thinning grey hair has been restored to her former "gleaming locks"- reminding us that she had violated her own honour when she gave the goblins a lock of her hair.

This brings the action to an **abrupt end- they all live happily ever after**- and what remains is an **epilogue of 25 lines** which presents the moral that there is a sisterhood (c.f. Rossetti's poem "Our Mothers, lovely women pitiful") which protects its members from the "deadly peril" of "poison in the blood" which is administered, not by goblins, but by "men".

On a superficial level, this story draws the childlike moral conclusion that mothers will keep their children safe, because they understand the dangers inherent in the outside world; but it mentions only sisters, not brothers. It may, to a Victorian adult, allude to **the Christian congregation as a source of support and collective strength in the fight against sin and the devil- if the Church is the Bride of Christ.**

It is purely speculation that there was an incident in Christina Rossetti's adolescence (it could have been the sermons of the Oxford Movement) which prompted her to mortify her own curiosity about sex (perhaps taking her cue from her older sister). It is perfectly possible that, turning 30, she still anticipated that she and her sister would marry and have daughters of their own.

Interpretation

This poem presents us, as contemporary readers, with a range of interpretative nuances. The narrative language of the poem is simple, as befits a story told as a sort of fairy-tale; there is a good deal of repetition of key words and phrases, the trajectory is that of a fairy story, and the use of images is fairly straightforward. When the beleaguered Lizzie is compared with a "fruit-crowned orange tree/ White with blossoms honey-sweet", it is an easier, healthier tree than the one in "An Apple Gathering".

While Rossetti is capable of writing short poems which praise virtue, the fact that this poem is so long implies that it is concerned with more complex ideas.

The idea that Lizzie and Laura are in fact two sides of the same personality anticipates the questions of psychoanalysis raised by Freud and Jung after about 1910 and explored in RL Stevenson's "Jekyll and Hyde" (1886). "Goblin Market" was written in 1859 and published in 1862.

Parts of the poem to do with the behaviour of the goblins and the consumption of the fruit are strikingly intense in their descriptive force. Is Lizzie subjected to a gang sexual assault? Is the consumption of the fruit and the concepts of shame/sin which apply to it such that Rossetti is alluding to sexual behaviour between men and women and to female orgasm? **Rossetti told her publisher that the poem was not intended for children, contradicting what she and her brother said in public.** She may have wanted to avoid any public scandal by leaving readers to form their own judgments in private.

As with all texts, you should be cautious about interpretations which distort the overall importance of themes which may appear tangentially in the poem. I doubt that Laura and Lizzie are lesbians, or that calling the poem "Goblin Market" makes it a Marxist tract because the title defines the focus of the poem as the activity of commerce. The strongest theme, we could argue, is raised by the **religious language**.

We know that Rossetti was working as **a volunteer in an institute for "fallen women" (prostitutes) from 1859 to 1870- the St Mary Magdalene house of charity in Highgate.** Its purpose was to help former prostitutes to acquire the social skills which would enable them to work as housemaids and integrate them into the ethos of the Church of England. Laura (who shares her name with Petrarch's romantic heroine) is presented as a girl who lacks the moral strength to resist a sensory temptation, and Jeanie appears to have died because she was accursed by her indulgence in pre-marital sex.

Laura does not need to be rehabilitated or forgiven; she needs to be helped back to physical and spiritual health, to a kind of pre-Fall innocence.

The poem works as a social critique of Victorian society's moral snobbery- its disapproval of "fallen women", whom that very society had failed, in the first place, in its morality, its education and its behaviour. Without goblins, there would be no prostitutes!

Rossetti's poems, taken as a whole, share a preoccupation with the difficulties women in particular experience in trying to fulfil their potential and achieve lasting satisfaction and happiness in a society which exploits and patronises them in various ways.

Here **the sisters live an ordered, conscientious but dull life of housekeeping- it has no art, no culture, no intellectual stimulation, no men- and so they are easily tempted by the first casual opportunity they encounter,** regardless of how dangerous it is. Laura cannot resist; she and Jeanie may perhaps have contracted syphilis or some other STD- which takes us back to William Blake's critique of English society, and the vulnerability of women driven into prostitution, in "London" (1794).

Winter- My Secret

This poem originally had the title "Nonsense", which implies that **there is no secret** to disclose.

The irregular form of the poem (four stanzas of 6/16/5/7 lines) **is anarchic, uncooperative, wild, free-spirited- all qualities which match the persona of this narrator.**

The attitude in the first stanza is coquettish and moderately fierce; the denials (no...not....not) are like the jabbing of a finger. The justification for keeping the secret here is that it is too cold (lines 3, 10, 20, 12-17) and the addressee is "too curious".

The second stanza goes on to extend the idea that **the secret is well hidden**, by listing **multiple layers of cold-weather clothing.**

This implies that the speaker may be more inclined to reveal it at a warmer time of year. When we reach stanza 3, the revelation- or, not even that, but the promise to tell the secret- is deferred again, form March, April, May, again on the grounds that the weather may be wintry and cold. If that were a valid excuse over the winter (and it isn't; it's just an arbitrary criterion of the narrator's choosing) it is a flimsy one because by the end of May the occasional cold spell is very much the exception.

The final stanza introduces the language of warm summer and autumn weather (languid/ drowsy/ golden/ ripening to excess/ sun/warm wind) and still makes the disclosure conditional on there being subjective judgments- who can say what "too much" sun or cloud means? Only the keeper of the secret.

The focus throughout is on the narrator's capricious, teasing attitude, until the very last line, when it suddenly shifts to the addressee, whom the narrator challenges to "guess"- you can trace the focus by looking at the pattern of the pronouns all the way through the poem.

The imagery of pecking or nipping combines with language of a type Rossetti uses when she wants to amuse, or write in a child-like way. There are some extremely simple and apparently transparent rhymes- froze/ blows/ snows/knows/ shows- and they are extended throughout the poem.

The use of words ending in -ing (nipping/ biting/ whistling/ bounding/ surrounding/ buffeting/ astounding/ nipping/ clipping/ ripening) is very reminiscent of the descriptions of the goblins in "Goblin Market"- it generates **a sense of movement, restlessness**, dynamism.

The overall process of the poem is to argue "I won't tell you my secret because it's too cold; I may impose other weather criteria, to keep it secret; there may not even be a secret; you might guess it if you really are curious enough". It is **built on contrasts** between cold and warmth, winter and summer, today and some day, secret and no secret, tell and won't tell, sunless and too much sun.

The mood and tone of the poem is playful rather than confrontational. If there is a more serious point here, it is that, once again, we have a female narrator who finds a voice and manages to assert that, **at least in one small corner of her life, she has discretion and control.** Throughout these poems, women who are denied a voice (most clearly in "From the Antique") are dispirited, while women who have a voice (Nell and some of the narrators) are as lively and interesting as any of the men.

Narrators who, as here and in "No, Thank you, John", exhibit wit, spirit, and a touch of defiant independence are not upstarts, but they engender respect; when they do speak for themselves, they do not seem less intelligent or educated than men (although in the real world education for girls was very rare, because the concept of a woman's place being in the home was so strong).

Soeur Louise de la Misericorde

There is a group of poems among Rossetti's output which return to the theme of renouncing worldly pleasure and temptation in favour of a reflective and devotional life; you may like to read "A Testimony", "The Lowest Room" and "One Certainty". She herself had a strong feeling of this kind while she was an adolescent, and her sister Maria became a nun in 1873.

The narrator here is the character of the Duchess de la Valliere, the mistress of Louis X1V, who entered a convent in 1675. Rossetti's longish poem "The Convent Threshold" expands on the seriousness this decision requires; it is a cutting off from what most people regard as the essential aspects of being a human being- a renunciation of all worldly things.

Soeur Louise is, presumably, an extreme example of someone who has lived amid luxury if not debauchery. There is nothing worth knowing about pleasure which she does not know herself.

Of the twenty lines in the poem, five are an **identical refrain** ("Oh vanity of vanities, desire"). The words desire/desired appear nine times, including the strategic final word. Rossetti uses **alliteration with words starting with the letter d, so that we associate desire with "days over/ dust/dying/ disenkindled/ deathbed/ dross/death-struck"- all processes which end without life or value.**

Other alliteration (life/longing/love/pangs/perished pleasure/plot/mock/memory/ mire/ measure) **and the repetition of key words** (love/life/longing/ fire) are designed to **create a fervour which is intensely emotional rather than merely rhetorical.**

But the real force lies less in the language of this poem than in the imagery- the fire with its dying embers, a memory like a swamp, love (paradoxically) as a fountain of sad tears and, personified, on its death-bed, bleeding drops not of blood but of "spent desire" which is now worthless "dross", and the speaker's life, symbolised as a rose which has "gone all to prickles" in a barren garden.

These images will prompt you to think of other poems- dross and fire in "Twice"; the garden in "Shut Out"; the drops of blood in "Good Friday".

Although stanza three signals a movement from contemplation of the past to contemplation of the present, the whole poem is a meditation on what the narrator now sees as a frivolous and wasted life.

The aesthetics of pain demand that the poem stays suspended in this state of mind; the same technique applies in "Good Friday" and "Uphill", where **the reader experiences self-reproach, fatigue and uncertainty.** Rossetti uses the imperfections or awareness of our human weakness to suggest that we really do need the transfiguration which religious belief engenders, and which she articulates in the latter part of "Twice".

In this poem **the lexis of death** (dying/ perished/ tears/ death-bed/ death-struck) **embodies repentance, whereas in "Remember" it embodied oppression and hatred.** The rose is, here, a symbol of sin (which throttles sensual pleasure); in "A Rose Plant in Jericho" Rossetti uses it as "a rose of joy and happy love and peace".

For once, the gender of the narrator is less important in this poem, although we may reflect that men may be less inclined than women to cast such a self-critical eye on their pasts! The overall process of the poem, however, is **cathartic- it engages the reader in a vicarious cleansing**, without the pain of witnessing the death of our own love.

Appendix 1

Critical judgments

In her 1981 biography "Christina Rossetti" (Constable and Company Ltd, page 65), Georgina Battiscombe judges "When I am dead, my dearest" as "this plaintive, **enchanting song**, which reads more like a poetic exercise than an expression of heartfelt emotion" (page 65). My view is that this is only one (the less important one) of two concurrent meanings or readings- it misses, completely, the dimension of **the narrator's disenchantment**.

Christina Rossetti's brother William promulgated the view that her poetry was spontaneous and artless. He may have formed this impression from recurring discussions she had had with her other brother, Dante Gabriel, who urged her to work more diligently, to produce more poems; she would say that you cannot write through an effort of the will.

Her obituary in "The Times" focused on "the purity of thought and diction" in her prose work "Commonplace" of 1870, her devotional writing, her "earnest religious convictions" and her "devotion to her aged mother". It compares her poetry unfavourably with her brother's, and **accuses her poetry of failing to create a "lasting impression", except for "Up-hill". It** judges "The Prince's Progress" better than "Goblin Market", which it does not comment on at all. It judges her poems as delicate, tender and sensitive- i.e. feminine- while conceding that the religious poems are "full of beauty and pathos", reflecting her secluded and "saintly" life.

This is a classic example of **a literary evaluation both shaped and spoiled by a perception of the writer's biography and gender**- it does not begin to seek any depth of meaning in the non-religious poems.

Literary critics in her own lifetime tended to look for **moral messages as a mark of superior art**, in a way which we simply do not. Ruskin said that great art always expresses **"moral law"** and FA Rudd wrote about the artist's obligation to show the reader **"moral right"**. The arrival of Modernism in the 1910s would weaken fatally this principle that personal behaviour must adhere to a cultural sense of morality, but- in criticism, if not in day to day life- Victorian critics see no shame in this.

Catholics found Rossetti's religious poems aesthetically appealing, while arguing that they would be even better if she were a member of their Church. Secular **critics of the time**, too, **expect to find conventional values being reinforced; they simply do not look for covert meaning or ambiguity.** The critic and poet Arthur Symons, writing on "Up-hill" (1858) in 1887, appreciated its "certainty" and the "relief" with which it contemplates (life after) death. He likes the sense of poems as prayers, and the absence of sermonising in them, so that they are personal utterances of "the soul's grief or joy". In 1896, Lionel Johnson attributes to Rossetti's Christianity the "tenderness……wistful beauty of adoration" she generates.

Victorian critics take the quiet orthodoxy of Rossetti's life as a green light to a view that the poems are pious and conventional; an appreciation of the frustrations, disappointments and existential doubt that came with it is beyond them. They are not attuned to irony or ambiguity, because they see Rossetti as a model of the Christian woman- humble, intensely devoted to God and family, passive, resigned, patient, submissive.

The idea that a woman could feel distress is alien to these critics, because of the culture they write in; never mind the unthinkably rebellious use of sonnets or ghost poems to express that distress.

The more socially and religiously inclined critics show little interest in "Goblin Market", criticising it for its blend of the surreal, the figurative, the adult and the child-like. Rather than accept the challenge to reinterpret their view of her poetry in the light of this bold and unorthodox, as well as ambitious, piece, **they choose to ignore it** (like the Times' obituarist).

The Edinburgh review (1893) called "Goblin Market" (published in 1862) grotesque and disproportionate; Edmund Gosse (in Century Magazine, 1893) approved of the grotesque, witty and fantastic aspects of the tale, and sought to extract a didactic meaning (not very successfully). Critics without religious affiliations are warmer towards the fantasy, the surrealism, the dream elements and the vividness of the imagery; **religious critics mistrust it**, as excessive, self-indulgent and Pre-Raphaelite. Christina Rossetti's death in 1894 more or less coincided with the start of Aestheticism, which would make the stricter religious critics less influential in shaping judgments about her.

Gender preconceptions are at work too, in these early critics. Harry Boxton Foreman mused (in Tinsley's Magazine", in 1869) that it is "impossible" for **women** to be eminent in the more serious or larger-scale forms of art, because their minds are "so differently fashioned from men's" that they **are incapable of "analysis and synthesis"** (a case, perhaps, of pots and kettles). Later, in articles from 1888 and 1899, the critic Amy Levy identified the qualities of Rossetti's voice as a poet ("curiously sweet, fantastically sad…..passionate….an imagination deep") and pointed out that women writers will tend to express more "personal feeling" than men in their writing.

Victorian critics criticised Rossetti for a lack of originality, although she breathes new life into the sonnet and the medieval romance; they would equally have criticised her for being too original, and one of the key criteria for placing her in the canon of (female) poets is, for these critics, relating her to her predecessors and contemporaries. This often leads to unfavourable comparisons with her brother simply on gender grounds- women's poetry has much less cultural value to the Victorians than men's (cf Robert and Elizabeth Barrett Browning).

Foreman **praises Rossetti's restraint, reticence and delicacy**. Edmund K Chambers approves of her **acceptance and resignation**. T Hall Caine (1881) associates Rossetti's state of resignation with truth, beauty and tenderness. Arthur Symons is better attuned to the "tragic ecstasy" and intense feeling in the poems, but he does not see it as a sign of distress.

The difference between artists and critics is that the artist seeks to break out of the cultural strictures of their life and times. **Critics- not just Victorians- too often use art to justify and reinforce their own values and preconceptions,** where they should be allowing themselves to be challenged. In hindsight, Rossetti might have felt that there was no need to code her pleas for equality and honesty in ambiguous forms, because the critics of her time were tuned to an entirely different wavelength.

In 1906, William Michael Rossetti's "Memoir" revealed his sister's two refusals to marry. The end of the Victorian age ushered in Modernism, and had to adjust to Darwin's theory of evolution (which called into question creationism and many of the old certainties), and the start of modern psychology (Jung and Freud) with its theories that the artist perhaps has less complete control over his material than had been supposed, because dreams and archetypal story patterns may be at work.

Oscar Wilde (1854-1900) and the aesthetic movement had changed the profile of writers, so that critics would find it more difficult to detach the writing from the life. Then, out of the First World War, came Modernism; a literary movement which sought to adjust to **the sense of individual insignificance,** and treated narrative in a more oblique way than before.

If you studied Priestley's "An Inspector Calls" for GCSE, you will remember how silly Mr Birling looks, in his complacent belief that nothing dangerous exists, and that Victorian manners and morality (and hypocrisy) can still govern a fast-changing world in which science and automation are breaking new ground every day.

Critics were now less likely to focus exclusively on the religious poems, and a school of thought emerges which seeks to explain the intensity of Rossetti's religious feeling and her renunciation of the pleasures of life not in doctrinal terms (the influence of the Oxford Movement) but as the sublimation of her personal unhappiness; dissatisfaction in our personal relationships can be compensated for, in the after life in Heaven- an extreme case of **deferred gratification**.

Virginia Woolf commented on Rossetti's humour in 1932; the idea that the ascetic and serious-minded poetess lived in an oasis of spiritual calm was being modified by the (still limited) biographical information which was emerging as time went on. **The principle that literature is created from personal experience is very different from the Victorian concept that art must teach morality, and in particular the conservative social morality of its time.**

The development of psychoanalysis leads critics to pay more attention to **symbolism and the allegorical quality** of some of the poems- Goblin Market, The Prince's Progress, Sleep at Sea, A Ballad of Boding, and to the possible underlying (unconscious) influence of myth and anthropology, which had come to the fore as a deliberate literary device in TS Eliot's "The Waste Land" (1922).

Christina Rossetti's biographer Jan Morris uses Freud's theories to construct **a theory that she was sexually abused by her father in about 1842; this is an attempt to explain her breakdown** and some of the more grotesque elements in some of the poems, as well as the recurring trope of keeping secrets. It is too complex a topic to explore here, but it exemplifies how new critical considerations affect critical thought and the need to **be clear about how far we think biographical fact and speculation are helpful in interpreting a writer's work** ("Christina Rossetti- A Literary Biography", Jonathan Cape, 1994).

A critical re-evaluation of the criteria for judging poetry led a significant number of critics between 1910 and 1940 to elevate Rossetti above Elizabeth Barrett Browning as the leading Victorian woman poet, because of the **emotional intensity, the lack of reticence, which frightened the Victorians in its immodesty, and because of Rossetti's lack of didacticism, which the Victorian critics had seen as a weakness.**

At last, we see a recognition of ambiguity in 1940, with FL Lucas's analysis of "Up-hill" not as a promise of Heaven (which, as we know, exists in the poem only in the minds of critics who go beyond the text) but as an Anglo-Saxon grave poem which leads us to the house of death.

The critic Susan Conley shares my sense that Rossetti uses language and nudges to the reader (rather than form) to subvert orthodoxy- in both the cold reality of death and the cruel coldness of the Victorian institution of marriage. She points out that superficial readings of "Remember" still persist, because they are "overdetermined by the prevalent biographical myth of Rossetti as a meek, deferential Victorian spinster" ("Rossetti's cold women", page 269, "The Culture of Christina Rossetti", ed Arseneau, Harrison and Kooistra, Ohio University press, 1999).

In recent decades, **(too) much critical effort has been devoted to linking various poems with what is known of Rossetti's life and relationships.**

 In my view, this is **a naïve approach which tends to underestimate writers' ability to draw on their imaginative powers.** No-one would say that the dramatic monologue, from Robert Browning onwards, reflects the poet's own life; and **poets use archetypes and different narrative voices to universalise elements of their own experience.** Poetry is rarely just a personal history, and **to seek to relate it above all to the poet's biography neglects the important issue of what the poem says to us.**

"Goblin Market" is fertile ground for these various critical perspectives. Rossetti denied that it had any moral or allegorical content, but, some critics argue, the power of **the subconscious** myth (self-sacrifice) may naturally be obscure to her. Others see it as an **allegorical criticism of Victorian attitudes to female sexuality, or to materialism.** Some critics see the two sisters as the writing out of **two irreconcilable sides of Rossetti's own personality**- the other-worldly, saintly one, and the one who would like to be fully involved in the real world of sensation and sex. The challenge for the critic is to **focus on the text** and not on preconceptions about what makes for a more (or less) valid critical approach.

The next critical focus, after the psychanalytical, is the **feminist**. This recognises that the poems are **produced at a certain time in a certain culture and that being female in that culture shapes their purpose and meaning.**

This raises the key interpretative question about Rossetti; is she an accepter of the status quo and of the social lot of women, or a protester, an insurgent, a revolutionary?

Appendix 2

Christina Rossetti's life

Born: 05.12.1830

Full name: Christina Georgiana Rossetti

Parents : Gabriele Rossetti (father) and Frances Rossetti (mother).

Gabriele Rossetti had been Curator of Antique Bronzes and Marbles in the Naples Museum. He left Italy as a political exile, settled in London in 1824 as a single man and eventually became Professor of Italian at King's College London. He was nominally a Roman Catholic but he had no strong religious views. In 1826 he married Frances Polidori; she was 17 years younger than him, and a strong member of the Church of England.

In 1843 ill-health forced Christina's father give up his job. He died in 1854.

Her mother died in 1886; this had a profound and negative effect on Christina who was 56 but had lived with her mother for all of her life.

Her siblings:

Maria Francesca (1827 – 1876.) Also an author, but gave this up to become a nun in 1876.

Gabriel Charles Dante (1828- 1882). The most famous in the family. Widely known as Dante Gabriel. Became a painter. Christina sat as a model for him. In 1848 he established the Pre-Raphaelite Brotherhood, a group of seven men, including James Collinson, who would later propose to Christina. Around 1849 he met the angelic poet and artist Lizzie Siddal, whom Christina Rossetti describes in her poem ,"In an Artist's Studio". They married in 1860, but she died in 1862, probably by deliberately poisoning herself. Following this, his health deteriorated over several years until his death.

William Michael. (1829 -1919). A writer and critic. Married late in 1875 at age 46, having lived with his mother and Christina since his father's death.

Whilst the sons went to school, the daughters were educated at home. It was a bookish family. Christina was fond of "The Arabian Knights" and Keats. William observed that Christina's two drives were love of her family and her own religious commitment. The family was influenced in its religion by the Oxford Movement. As an adolescent, Christina attended sermons by William Dodsworth and became an Anglo- Catholic in her outlook.

Key events

Something significant but not known affected Christina psychologically between 1842 and 1847; she became very shy, and ascetic in her approach to life. The illness of her father and the influence of the Oxford Movement may have been contributing factors.

In 1848, when she was 18, James Collinson proposed to her, but she rejected him because he had become a Roman Catholic. He reverted to Anglicanism and she accepted, but he returned to Catholicism two years later. Christina must have felt that his religious point of view was more important to him than she was; her brother William described the episode as "a staggering blow at her peace of mind".

The poem "No, Thank you, John" was written in 1860, and Christina denied that it was based on a real person, but her brother William said that it referred to an incident with the painter John Brett in about 1852. Christina's pencil note saying that "the original John was obnoxious" supports William's view.

Her grandparents died in 1853 (her grandfather was over 90).

In or after 1862 she developed a friendship with Charles Cayley, who had been a student of her father's- her poem "A Sketch" is about him. He eventually asked her to marry him (probably in 1866) but she felt he was not sufficiently religious. They remained friends until his death in 1883. It may be that her serious ill-health in 1864 inhibited her from marrying him; she had a better diagnosis in April 1865 and then made a trip to Italy. Eventually, after long reflection, she concluded that she could not marry a man whose appreciation of God was weak or absent. Ultimately the fervour of her religious sensibility was so strong that no human relationship could provide comparable or complementary meaning for her.

In 1871 she suffered from Graves' disease and stopped writing for a while. In the later 1880s she wrote poetry but did not publish it. She wrote religious prose for the SPCK (Society for Promoting Christian Knowledge).

In 1892 she had surgery for breast cancer, became progressively less and less active, and died on 29/12/1894.

Development as a writer

Christina wrote verse from the age of 12; in 1847 her grandfather printed her early poems, to distribute them among the Rossetti circle. Her health was poor between 1843 and 1852; according to William, this made her conscious in her outlook, more or less all the time, of death and morbidity.

1850- she had seven poems published in the short-lived Pre-Raphaelite magazine The Germ. The first edition sold only 200 copies and it soon folded.

1854- the poems she was writing included "Remember" and "Song- When I am dead, my dearest".

1855- Rossetti has a further bout of ill-health- possibly angina, or consumption. At the end of the year she worked as a governess, but her health again made this only a short-term possibility.

1856- Writes "In an Artist's Studio", about her brother and Lizzie Siddal, whom he finally married in 1860. Two of her poems from 1857 may allude to her secret regard for Charles Cayley.

1862- Publication of "Goblin Market and other Poems" (by Macmillan), who had already published "Up-hill", "A Birthday" and "An Apple Gathering". Ruskin had criticised "Goblin Market" for its irregular verse forms. She had worked on it since 1860;

from 1860 to 1870 she volunteered at the House of Charity at Highgate, an institution run by Anglican nuns, which rehabilitated prostitutes and other abandoned and destitute women. This has an influence on "Goblin Market" and on some of her other major poems- "Cousin Kate" and "Under the Rose" (1865- retitled in 1872 as "The Iniquity of the Fathers upon the Children").

1864- She appeared to be suffering with tuberculosis which was potentially fatal but she wrote 14 poems that year.

1866- publication of "The Prince's Progress"; the poem which gives the collection its title is a long narrative poem, like "Goblin Market". It addresses Ruskin's concerns but does not benefit from either that point or Dante Gabriel's editorial interference. The collection omits "Twice", although she had written it in 1864.

1872- published "Sing-Song" (verse for children).

1881 Published "A Pageant and other Poems".

Appendix 3

Women's rights

Victorian legislation was slow to react, but it eventually reinforced social trends, without leading them. Women's rights were barely in existence when Rossetti wrote these poems.

Until 1857 (the Matrimonial Causes Act) women had no grounds for divorce, and then they had limited access to it, but only on the grounds of adultery plus one additional cause of incest/bigamy/cruelty/ desertion.

Domestic violence- which had been a persistent issue- was finally recognised as a potential justification for divorce.

Women whose marriages had ended in separation had very limited access to their children. The 1839 Custody of Infants Act permitted access to mothers of unblemished character, but it was only in the 1870s that mothers' access to their children was extended much, that there was a presumption that fathers should support their children financially and that married women were legally entitled to keep their earnings.

Domestic violence was a largely unspoken of evil but legislation was needed, leading to the Act for the Better Prevention and Punishment of Aggravated Assaults upon Woman and Children (1853).

By contrast, proposed legislation to protect prostitutes failed to be passed in the 1840s. In Rossetti's time, the age of consent for girls was 12; it only rose to 16 in 1885. Legislation between 1864 and 1869 allowed the police to conduct forced examinations for evidence of sexually transmitted diseases on any woman suspected of prostitution.

The Pre-Raphaelite Movement

This was a small society of artists, founded in 1848 and driven by Dante Gabriel Rossetti. It no longer existed formally after 1853. A second wave of art adhering to its theories followed in the 1860s and afterwards.

He enlisted his fellow painters Holman Hunt and Millais (they were all students at the Royal Academy of Art). Their belief was that artists post-Raphael had sacrificed a style of pre-Renaissance painting which should be preserved, with its emphasis on nature, truth, beauty, simplicity and symbolism, and bright colouring. Among their aims, as defined by William Rossetti, was the principle of being attuned to "what is direct and serious and heartfelt in previous art, to the exclusion of what is conventional"; it was a protest against the artificial and mannered. Realism and symbolism are difficult to combine, and their avowed interest in depicting Nature accurately was far removed from the style of medieval painting which they admired for its emotional intensity.

The other members were William Rossetti, James Collinson (Christina's fiancé), FG Stephens (another painter and critic) and the sculptor T Woolner.

Their publication "The Germ" attracted little interest. Their values prompted debate – Ruskin supported them while Dickens thought their style ugly, primitive and even blasphemous.

The Oxford Movement

Among the theologians at the heart of this movement in the Church of England were Newman, Pusey and Keble. Its principles became known as Tractarianism, named after its publications between 1833 and 1841. These theologians were based in Oxford University. Newman became a Roman Catholic in 1845 and later became a Cardinal.

In 1833, Keble raised concerns about legislation which would weaken the established Anglican Church in Ireland. He and his colleagues objected to what they saw as a liberalising and dumbing down of the traditional manners and liturgy of the

Church of England and they sought to align it more with the Roman Catholic Church.

Many of the priests who sympathised with this Anglo-Catholic doctrine were assigned to parishes in slums, where they tried to deal with cholera epidemics and the social consequences of poverty and deprivation. Frances Rossetti started attending one such church in 1843, and it is likely that Christina heard sermons by some of the leading figures in the movement; the message was about the evil of sin, the emptiness of life in this world and the vision of Heaven as a place of grace and blessing.

In this version of High Anglicanism, women were encouraged to dedicate themselves to God, and Anglican nunneries became established, locally, in 1845. This was when Christina became ill; she was judged to be suffering from "religious mania" and her social withdrawal, and the emotionalism of her religious poetry, reflects the influence her mother exposed her to.

Religious Influence

Given the difficulty inherent in uniting Anglican and Roman Catholic traditions, it is perhaps understandable that (as in Shakespeare) not all of Rossetti's poems adopt the same vision of death.

In some Christian traditions, the soul has to undergo a form of purgatory before it can ascend to Heaven- this is the context we find in Shakespeare's "Hamlet". If the soul does not go straight to Heaven (as Macbeth thinks Duncan's does, in "Macbeth"), because the Last Judgment brings the dead back to life (as the Book of Revelation which concludes the Bible has it), the soul must be in a state of suspension until then; this is a doctrine sometimes referred to as "soul sleep".

Because Rossetti is writing in different tones and moods, we should not expect her to adhere in all of her poems to a single view; inconsistency is a necessary artistic freedom in this area.

Sample Essay

"Forbidden tastes are sweetest"; consider how Christina Rossetti explores the attraction of what is forbidden.

Christina Rossetti's poetry often presents thwarted desire; sometimes it is out of reach because of other people's behaviour, and sometimes it is out of bounds- in which case, it is not necessarily out of reach.

The forbidden fruit in "Goblin Market" symbolises female curiosity about sex. The figure of Jeanie is a warning that experimenting with sex outside or before marriage is fatal; it makes you a fallen woman. Several aspects of the characterisation in this poem are provocative. The goblins, who are men, set out to humiliate "maids" through a sexual initiation which resembles gang rape. They seduce maids by alluring them with the fruit which is impure and transmits disease (sexually).

Sexual experience is disorientating for both Laura and Lizzie- it leaves them not knowing whether it is night or day- and it is addictive. But the goblins are no longer accessible after sex so there is no chance of any repeat.

The meaning here is complex because it conflates female desire with irresponsible male behaviour; something is being said about sexual morality, with men being permitted to use young girls as prostitutes (although they do not pay them), devaluing them in the marriage market and abandoning them. Jeanie and Laura are "fallen women"; Rossetti uses the analogy of Eve in the Garden of Eden to convey the sheer force of their curiosity and the allure of what is forbidden. Her real point is that men are responsible for the sexual corruption of young women who become outcasts because as unmarried mothers or prostitutes they have no legal protection or rights (the law did not catch up with this social problem until the 1870s, because men were reluctant to legislate in a way which ceded power to women).

The theme of authoritarian men depriving women of what was once permitted to them dominates "Shut Out", where it is unclear why the narrator has been expelled from her garden. Again, there is an inexact parallel, perhaps, with the Garden of Eden. This narrator associates the garden from which she is now excluded as a type of Paradise. It is fertile and febrile with growth. The silent gatekeeper systematically destroys the view so that the narrator cannot derive any comfort from it. The garden is a symbol of a happier, more natural life in which emotional stimuli were happy, not sad. The allegory here may be of a woman's life before and after marriage; having left the garden of innocence, she will never be as happy again, and the legal impossibility of divorce even after 1857 for most women means that marriage is a watershed which cuts women off from the happiest times of their lives.

"From the Antique" makes the point that female distress is not only domestic; the patriarchal values of Victorian society (and societies older than that) exclude women from education, public life and positions of influence. Remarkably, this nameless, archetypal female narrator longs for oblivion- being "nothing at all"- as the cure for her sense of her own insignificance. She does not define herself as a mother, and the poem omits the issue of whether motherhood confers some status or respectability on women; this omission suggests that, for the purpose of this poem, it does not. It is not just a deficit in power between the genders which the poem articulates- forbidding women a voice and a role excludes them from any sense of personal fulfilment or satisfaction. So long as education is virtually confined to boys and men, there will be no generational change in this inequality of opportunity. "I wish I were a man", the narrator says, not in order to oppress women, but to make an impression so that "the world" (wider society) would be aware of and interested in what she had to say.

Much of Rossetti's poetry is about the voicelessness of women and their exclusion from happiness and fulfilment both in marriage ("Remember Me", "Song-when I am dead, my dearest", "Shut Out") and in wider society ("From the Antique"). The fallen woman- Maude Clare, Laura, Jeanie- is exploited too. Rossetti's women retaliate by threatening to haunt the men who have wronged them after they die, and by keeping secrets ("Winter; my secret"); or ("Twice") by removing themselves from blaming men and devoting themselves to God instead.

When they are not forbidden to speak, Rossetti's women, whether they are the narrators of the poems, or Nell in "Maude Clare", demonstrate a capacity for incisive thinking and for generosity which makes their exclusion the more regrettable.

Women will have to find their own voice in their homes and marriages; but "Goblin Market" addresses the wider social issue of how "fallen women" deserve to be rehabilitated instead of condemned. While the goblin fruit is presented as an illusion or a perversion- twice, the narrator stresses that such fruit is not to be found in any real market in the real world- the shaming and exploitation of "maids" is very real, and the poem is a contribution towards seeing the female point of view in a world where law and morality is shaped by men for their own convenience.

Gavin Smithers is a private tutor based in Chipping Campden, Gloucestershire. He has an English degree from Oxford University, and a passion for helping students to discover the joy and satisfaction of great literature.

So….if there's anything you're not sure about and your teacher can't help, please do contact the author- grnsmithers@hotmail.co.uk

Gavin's Guides are short books packed with insight. Their key aim is to help you raise your grade. For full details, look up Gavin's author page on Amazon.co.uk

Other titles include:

Understanding Arthur Miller's All My Sons. Understanding J.B. Priestley's An Inspector Calls. Understanding George Orwell's Animal Farm. Understanding William Golding's Lord of the Flies. Understanding Charles Dickens' Great Expectations. Understanding John Steinbeck's Of Mice and Men. Understanding Emily Dickinson's Set Poems. Understanding Edward Thomas' Set Poems. Understanding Harper Lee's To Kill A Mockingbird. Understanding Andrew Marvell's Cromwell & Eulogy Poems. Understanding Poems of the Decade for A level Edexdcel Poetry. Understanding Kazuo Ishiguro's Never Let Me Go. Understanding Jerusalem by Jez Butterworth Understanding Philp Larkin's "The Whitsun Weddings" for A Level Students

Printed in Great Britain
by Amazon